Jeff B. Crouse

YOUR *New*
IDENTITY

*Taking care of your half
of the whole*

Your New Identity
Taking Care of Your Half of the Whole
By: Jeff B. Crouse

Library of Congress Control Number: 2010942358

Publisher's Cataloging-in-Publication data
(Provided by Adrienne Bashista Cataloger-at-large)

Crouse, Jeff B.
    Your new identity : taking care of your half of the whole / Jeff B. Crouse.
    p. cm.
    ISBN 978-0-9827446-2-8
    Includes bibliographical references.

1. Identification (Religion) --Biblical teaching. 2. Identity (Psychology). 3. Faith --Biblical teaching. 4. Spiritual life --Christianity. 5. Christian life. I. Title.

BS2655.I33 .C76 2011
233/.5 –dc22

2010942358

This book is printed on acid-free paperand meets ANSI Z39.48 standards

Scripture quoted, unless otherwise noted, is from the King James Version (KJV).

Manufactured in America

Jacket Design: Rodrigo Aguilera
Edited by: Gary Peterson

Omaha, NE

Table of Contents

Preface   7
Introduction   11

Chapters
Don't Bury Your Talents   21
Self Mastery   27
Seek God First   35
Identity   39
Our Mind   49
Imagination   55
Emotions   61
Our Ego   75
Physical Health   79
Words   97
Wisdom   113
The Purpose of Life   121
Individual Purpose   125
Forget Your Past Failures   131

Preface

Like newborn babies, crave pure spiritual milk, so that by it you may grow up in your salvation, now that you have tasted that the Lord is good.
1 Peter 2:2-3 (NIV).

Jesus called them together and said, "You know that the rulers of the Gentiles lord it over them, and their high officials exercise authority over them. Not so with you. Instead, whoever wants to become great among you must be your servant, and whoever wants to be first must be your slave—just as the Son of Man did not come to be served, but to serve, and to give his life as a ransom for many.
Matthew 20:25-28 (NIV).

Writing and teaching is not necessarily about telling people something they have never heard. Rather than teaching, I prefer to call it sharing. We all are created in the Image of God, yet we are all created different from each other. Each one of us is unique; we each have a very unique way of seeing things. When we write, teach, or share, it is not always something that the reader or listener has never heard, but when we share it as our own experience, it may be that they are receiving an old story in a new way.

When we have been enlightened and our eyes are suddenly opened to something new, we need to retain this new information. We were once blind, but now through Christ we see. What do we see? We see his word and the world around us in a completely new way. We can now knock and begin to see behind open doors that were once closed. As we seek, we will find. What will we find? We will find a new way of life; we will find new truths that God has inlaid into his word. These new truths are revealed to us by God: we need to remember them and retain them in our "memory closet" for future use. God reveals to us and he opens our eyes to new things because this new information has a purpose. It helps us to grow and it will stimulate new growth in others. The best way to remember what we learn is to share. When we who are sharing tell others what we've learned. Whether through writing or the spoken word, it not only should be edifying to them, but also to the one doing the sharing. In addition, the more we retell the good news, the more engrained in us it becomes; thereby helping our own growth as much as the listener or the reader. Sharing new insights or sharing something that has been revealed to us from God is not always about helping the other person: sometimes it's about helping ourselves.

Being a teacher or a leader doesn't mean you are smarter than anyone else, or that you know something that the listener has never contemplated. There are times when we share our knowledge, or teach our knowledge to others as we are also realizing these truths for the first time ourselves. Talking about it helps us to become more convinced of it. Sharing a new idea or thought, or an experience, helps the one who is listening, but it also is helping the one doing the sharing.

If someone is telling you something and they are all excited about it, but you have heard it a million times already; don't be so quick to stifle their message or their words. It's not about you, it's about them. They need to tell you these things, because it is more beneficial to their growth and development than yours is at this particular time. Who knows, it may lead into conversation that covers ground you never considered, thereby you both walk away enlightened. When a child discovers an airplane in the sky for the first time, or sees a butterfly; you don't roll your eyes and treat them as if that is silly. You share in their excitement as if you are also discovering for the first time that plane, or that butterfly—though you've seen each of them a million times. When we do this we both walk away happy, both the child and the adult. Sometimes as adults, we can be childlike with new knowledge, wanting to share it with everybody we know. If someone does this to you, let them speak. When you allow the other person to share with you something that is new to them, or something that the Lord has recently put on their heart; you are contributing to their growth whether or not you get anything out of it. This process is about the renewing of our mind, both yours and theirs.

When I write I hope and pray that someone else will be blessed by it, but it is always building me up as well. To share my thoughts helps me to grow and helps me to remember better the new knowledge with which I've been blessed.

There are no new truths where God is concerned, yet when we learn something new or when our eyes are opened to a new truth for us, it draws us closer to him. This makes God happy to see us grow and learn. When our children first discover a new word or take their first step, we celebrate with them and get just as excited as they do, even though we have said millions of words and taken millions of steps.

When we step out of our comfort zone, when we stretch ourselves, when we grow and move beyond where we've already been, God shares in our joy just as we share the joy with our children when they do the same.

This excitement and rejoicing at the accomplishments of others is how we as believers should be with one another. I have friends who will share with me some new insight they have into a Bible story I've already read a hundred times. In the past there have been times when I didn't want to listen, but as the storyteller talked I began to realize they were telling an old story, but in a new and amazing way. They are telling it from their point of view and I always walk away blessed.

Why is it that we can get so excited over such minor things with our children? Why is it that God rejoices over us when we discover something that he knew about all along? Because of love; we love our children and God loves us. We as Christian brothers and sisters should love each other the same way.

When it comes to some new knowledge the Lord has blessed us with, we have to guard against our ego. Teaching one another scripture and sharing new information is a form of serving one another. It doesn't mean, "I am smarter than you," or "you are closer to God than me." It's about laying aside our ego and serving God by serving others; whether you are the one doing the talking or the listening, the writing or the reading, the giving or the receiving, it does not matter. Each is equally important. In Matthew 20:26b-28 (NIV), Jesus said, "...whoever wants to become great among you must be your servant, and whoever wants to be first must be your slave—just as the Son of Man did not come to be served, but to serve, and to give his life as a ransom for many." This can only be done with love in your heart and mind, if you are not coming from a place of true love, it will not last.

Our struggle is not one that should be fought day to day; but moment-to-moment. Sharing, fellowship and pouring from vessel to vessel is a major weapon in our warfare.

My prayer is that through this book God will open your eyes to some new ideas and concepts, even though I address topics you may have already heard or read about many times. One thing is for certain, by writing this book; I have experienced tremendous growth in my own life. Over the course of this book as you read my words, I thank you for allowing me to share some of my thoughts and revelations with you. Right there is really what it's all about—my sharing with you and you sharing with others. As you read this book, I do not necessarily want you to believe as I do: I just want you to think, contemplate, meditate and draw closer to God. You will be able to add to my words, take away from my words. In the end my hope is that you'll get a picture of the true character and nature of God, which will in turn help you to achieve new growth. Just make sure you contribute to someone else's growth in exchange.

Introduction

He replied, I saw Satan fall like lightning from heaven.
Luke 10:18 (NIV).

How you are fallen from heaven,
O Lucifer,[a] son of the morning!
How you are cut down to the ground,
You who weakened the nations!
For you have said in your heart:

I will ascend into heaven,
I will exalt my throne above the stars of God;
I will also sit on the mount of the congregation
On the farthest sides of the north;
I will ascend above the heights of the clouds,
I will be like the Most High.
Isaiah 14:12-14 (NKJV)

As Christians, we understand and accept that Heaven is a perfect place; that in Heaven there is no sorrow, no sickness or pain. In Heaven, there is eternal life; because of the absence of sin, there is no death.

As Christians we also know and understand after the creation of the earth God made the Garden of Eden; he made every seed bearing plant come up out of the ground, along with all of the trees that were to be used for food. He then put the man in the Garden to tend it and the woman was placed there with him. In the Garden there was no sin, sickness, death, or disease. They were created to live forever, to experience eternal life and to have no wants, needs or any form of lack. God never intended man to experience different seasons of life. Man was created to live in an eternal state of well being. The creation was the springtime of humanity; like spring, everything was alive and blooming. Life was to beget life and we would never experience the summer, fall and winter of life [things like death, depression, sickness, disease and separation]. The only seasons God created us to experience were the seasons that come about ir nature, (*cf.* Gen. 1:14).

The Garden in a sense is a duplicate of Heaven. The Garden of Eden is a third dimensional, physical reflection o Heaven, which is in a higher dimensional spiritual realm; however both of these places are places of eternal life and perfection Isaiah 14:12-14 tells us in Heaven that Lucifer wanted to exal himself above God, to exalt himself above the stars of God.

In Genesis chapter three, we read how the woman was deceived by the serpent. She ate from the tree of the knowledge of good and evil only after he told her she could be like God. [Even here, we still see a parallel or a reflection between Heaver and the Garden.]

Both Lucifer and Eve [with Lucifer it was inherent, with Eve it was deception at this point; she had a choice] suffered from the same problems with which we fight to this very day. [It seems the more things change the more they stay the same.] They both had the thought first. In their mind they each desired to be exalted to a place that was equal to and above God himself. Their problems were character flaws, which we struggle with in daily life even now, pride, selfishness and arrogance. These thoughts cause some people today to try to form all of the right relationships with key people, to jockey for position in school, at work and even in church to exalt themselves above others.

This raises a couple of questions. We know that wickedness exist in our world because of sin, but if Heaven and the Garden were perfect places of peace, serenity and eternal life; is it possible that wickedness existed in both of them? And if so...why? Hold that thought; we will come back to these questions a bit later. First, we need to address something else.

God created us to live in eternal springtime, in eternal life, to never know death, sickness and disease. But as a result of mans sin death was brought into the world. Because he loves us and because his purpose for us will never fail, he took something, that Satan meant for evil and used it to bring us life once again.

He now uses death as the engine that drives life...death begets life.

Paraphrasing John 12:24, Jesus said that unless a seed falls into the ground and dies of itself, it will remain alone. In other words, if you purchase a package of seeds, take them home and put them on the counter; then come back in a year, five years, or ten years—they will still be only seeds. But put these seeds in the right environment and they will die to become what God purposed them to be. God designed a seed with DNA genetic code. A pumpkin seed will never grow into a tomato, a tomato seed will never grow into a stalk of corn. They will either remain a seed or become what God intended for them to be. As this seed grows it's slowly dying to what it once was, it's transforming and changing into its destiny. As this process takes place, it dies from a seed and gives life to a source of food, which in turn is plucked when the time is right; then dies to bring us life when we eat it. Everywhere you look, with humans and in nature, death begets life; an acorn dies to become a tree, a caterpillar dies, transforms and leaves behind what it is now to become a butterfly. In order to begin anything new, something must end.

When we are in the womb, we have to leave that life behind when we are born into this world. When we become a born again Christian we die to our old way of life as we pursue our new life with Christ. At some point, we experience a physical death, which is then followed by eternal life. Our lives are constantly going through changes. We consistently have to be transformed as we age. Some examples of these changes would be; when we marry, when we have children, when our children leave home, when we change careers or when we go through a serious illness or a divorce. Each of these examples will force us to experience an ending, but as a result, we will experience a new beginning as well.

If you look at creation as a canvas, you'll see that each day the artist added something new which changed the overall look of his beautiful creation. In the beginning the artist installed his canvas, but it was blank, it was void and without form. He then added some light and dark on the first day of work. Each day he added more, the sky, the oceans, the mountains and valleys. Plants and trees were added, then animals and finally man was brought forth. Each day this painting grew, nothing was lost; nothing had to be lost because there was only goodness and perfection. God added daily to his creation in order to bring it into what he had destined it to be. Once sin came into the world, death was introduced to us; now, as a result of sin, we have to leave things behind in order to move forward in life.

Everything God created was inside of him all along. He gave birth to man, the universe and everything in it. We all came from God and it seems that we spend our life looking, seeking and searching for happiness and a sense of belonging. Perhaps we are trying to find our way back home. We all have this deeply engrained desire to grow, to expand, to merge, to be a part of something. Some people turn to drugs, poor relationships, alcohol, pornography and sex to get acceptance: to fit in. Looking for some kind of happiness or escape from the troubles of the world. Because of the distractions of the world, few find their way back to the place they came from, "Small is the gate and narrow the road that leads to life...," (*cf.* Matt. 7:14 NIV)

Christians will enter into a series of life changing situations; the seventh and final is eternal life. Perhaps it could be called eternal Sabbath or rest. We enter into that place that was meant for us from the beginning. We enter into a time of menuha [menuha is the Hebrew word for rest] it is tranquility, peace and serenity. Rabbi Abraham Joshua Heschel says it like this from his book, The Sabbath:

> To the biblical mind *menuha* is the same as happiness and stillness and peace and harmony. The word with which Job described the state after life he was longing for is derived from the same root as menuha. It is the state wherein man lies still, wherein the wicked cease from troubling and the weary are at rest. It is the state in which there is no strife and no fighting, no fear and distrust. The essence of the good life is menuha. "The Lord is my shepherd, I shall not want, He maketh me to

lie down in green pastures; He leadeth me beside still waters." [the waters of menuhot] In later times menuha became a synonym for the life in the world to come, for eternal life.

He also goes on to say, "The meaning of the Sabbath is to celebrate time rather than space. Six days a week we live under the tyranny of things of space; on the Sabbath we try to become attuned to holiness in time. It is a day on which we are called upon to share in what is eternal in time, to turn from the results of creation to the mystery of creation; from the world of creation to the creation of the world.

God created us to live in eternal peace and serenity and this is where Adam and Eve started. Through sin, death was brought into the world. Jesus came as a seed for us and through his death God brought us eternal life. He laid down his life so that we could have life and have it more abundantly.

Jesus replied, "The hour has come for the Son of Man to be glorified. I tell you the truth, unless a kernel of wheat falls to the ground and dies, it remains only a single seed. But if it dies, it produces many seeds. The man who loves his life will lose it, while the man who hates his life in this world will keep it for eternal life. Whoever serves me must follow me; and where I am, my servant also will be. My Father will honor the one who serves me," (*cf.* John 12:23-26 NIV).

God loves us so much that he sent his son to die for us; he loves us so much that even death will not stop his plan for humanity. Satan meant death to be a bad thing for you and me, but God in his infinite wisdom now brings us life through death. His love for us is deeper than we can even imagine.

Now back to the questions we asked earlier, is it possible that wickedness existed in a perfect place? And if so, why? The answer to the first question would be yes, or it may be more accurate to say that the seed of it existed until Lucifer caused it to manifest. According to Isaiah, it was just a thought; it was not necessarily an act, but rather it was what he had in his heart and just the thought of it was enough to get him kicked out. The same thing happened in the Garden, Eve didn't actually speak out; she had a thought that led to the act of disobedience. The Bible only says that she saw it was good; she then ate the fruit, which contained the seed of knowledge of good and evil. When Adam and Eve took part in eating it the manifestation occurred. The serpent planted a seed in their mind in the form of a thought and they both had a choice whether to partake or not. It was not just Eve who brought this about; the word clearly tells us that she gave to the man who was there with her and he ate of it as well.

When God questioned Adam, Adam blamed it on the woman. When God confronted Eve, she blamed it on the serpent. Just like you and I they were afraid to take responsibility for their own actions, so they started finger pointing, putting the blame on one another and as a result Adam and Eve were banished from the garden and not allowed to return. The second question is why; why was this allowed to take place? The answer would have to be...love.

In order for perfect love to exist, there must be room for choices. For God to not allow us choices would not be perfected love. He could easily force us to follow him. He could easily force us to bow down and worship him too, but that would not be the relationship he desires to have with us. We are to love him because he first loved us, (*cf.* 1 John 4:19 paraphrased).

There are parents who try to control the lives of their adult children. They will threaten to banish them from the family if they don't obey. I've heard stories of parents who made statements like "if you marry her then you are no longer a part of this family!" or "if you marry him you will be disowned!" "You are no longer my daughter!" It becomes a battle of wills between the parents and children, eventually pride and ego will not allow them just to be conscious enough to see what is happening. This is not love on the part of the parents, although they think it is. Our sons and daughters at some point have to be able to have choices. To make their own decisions and mistakes as they go through life.

If we truly love them, we must have the awareness to know that forcing anything on another is not love and it creates a huge gap, a void. It opens sores that over time will fester leading to all sorts of other problems.

We are sons and daughters of God and he doesn't want to force his love on us. He gently calls us, he whispers to us with love and patience. As you read this, he is speaking to you now, wanting you to draw closer to him, to walk and live in his presence.

Just as a seed has to die to itself to become something more, we in turn have to do the same thing. We are to die to our old way of thinking, our old way of talking, die to our old way of life [our flesh]. We are to take our thoughts captive and make them obedient to the will of Christ; we are to daily be engaged in the renewing of our mind, allowing the old man to die making room for the new. We have within us a seed, within that seed is an embryo and within that embryo is the DNA for what God put inside of you and me before we were even born.

To seek first the kingdom of God, to grow and become better every day than you were the day before is to continually move into the life that Jesus desires you to have. Seeking God's kingdom is not for fame and fortune, but to win others to Christ. It's not by force, but through love, to bring him glory in all that you do. You don't have to try to become someone that you're not, you simply have to be you, not the false ego you carry around of who you think you're supposed to be.

Michelangelo, famous for his paintings, he considered himself more a sculptor than a painter. Someone once asked him how he could take raw marble and turn it into a beautiful sculpture. He said he didn't turn it into anything that it wasn't already; he could look at this big piece of marble and see the beautiful statue imprisoned within it. He would then simply chip away what was not needed, slowly, one day at a time releasing the creation that was trapped inside; eventually revealing something truly beautiful, majestic and eternal.

This is the way we are, we just need to chip away a little bit of our old self everyday. Allowing the baggage, negativity and insecurity, to just die; thus revealing our true self. God loves us and wants to take us by the hand and lead us on a wonderful journey through life. He wants to see us fulfill the purpose he has for us because of his love. We in turn have to love him in order to please him.

If we love God then we also love our brother, in order to love our brother we have to love ourselves. There is one rule that sums up all commandments, "love your neighbor as yourself," (*cf.* Matt. 19:19 NIV). If we hate ourselves it makes loving our fellow man impossible and if we don't love our brother who we have seen, then we can't love God who we haven't seen. If we love God and our brother then we will do the work to bring our life to a place of spiritual, mental and emotional maturity that will enable us to serve God by serving our neighbor, our brother. If we do not or can not love ourselves enough to mature in every area of our life, then what can we offer to those in need? What gifts and talents can we bring to the table?

Beloved, let us love one another, for love is of God; and everyone who loves is born of God and knows God. He who does not love does not know God, for God is love. In this the love of God was manifested toward us, that God has sent His only begotten Son into the world, that we might live through Him. In this is love, not that we loved God, but that He loved us and sent His Son to be the propitiation for our sins. Beloved, if God so loved us, we also ought to love one another. No one has seen God at any time. If we love one another, God abides in us, and His love has been perfected in us. By this we know that we abide in Him, and He in us, because He has given us of His Spirit. And we have seen and testify that the Father has sent the Son as Savior of the world. Whoever confesses that Jesus is the Son of God, God abides in him, and he in God. And we have known and believed the love that God has for us. God is love, and he who abides in love abides in God, and God in him. Love has been perfected among us in this: that we may have boldness in the day of judgment; because as He is, so are we in this world. There is no fear in love; but perfect love casts out fear, because fear involves torment. But he who fears has not been made perfect in love. We love Him because He first loved us. If someone says, "I love God," and hates his brother, he is a liar; for he who does not love his brother whom he has seen, how can he love God whom he has not seen? And this commandment we have from Him: that he who loves God must love his brother also. (*cf.* 1 John 4:7-21 NKJV).

You have a seed that was planted in you from the beginning and you'll be known to others by the fruit that you bear in life. Let's leave our flesh behind and follow after the spirit, by chipping away all of the unneeded and unwanted negative parts of our life. Let's grow spiritually, mentally and emotionally to the place where we can master sin by mastering ourselves; thereby multiplying the talents Christ left in our care when he went away. He is on a journey. He has gone to prepare a place for you and me; one day he will return.

He loves you so much that not even death can hinder his desire for you; now death brings life. His love for you allows for choices to be made. Show your love for God by making the right choices; which in turn brings glory and honor to him.

WHEN I STAND BEFORE GOD,
AT THE END OF MY LIFE,
I WOULD HOPE THAT I WOULD NOT
HAVE A SINGLE BIT OF TALENT LEFT,
AND COULD SAY,
I USED EVERYTHING YOU GAVE ME.

—Erma Bombeck

1
⇜Don't Bury Your Talents⇝

A man's gift makes room for him,
And brings him before great men.

Proverbs 18:16 NKJV

It was October 21, the weather outside was overcast as a cold front was north just a few days away. Honking geese could be heard as they flew south for the winter. The wind was gently blowing through the trees. Jack and his wife Elizabeth had decided to stay in bed today and spend some much needed time together. They lay there talking about life; about their hopes, dreams, goals and desires for the future. They were sharing a daily devotional together and studying the word of God. The room was dimly lit and the shades were drawn. Fresh brewed coffee was in the air. Some of Jack and Elizabeth's fondest memories were of mornings when they could share a cup of coffee and good conversation about the word of God. By this time, the hustle and bustle of life seemed a million miles away and they hadn't a care in the world as they lay there talking and sharing.

Jack recalled a profound insight about the grave shared by a minister named Myles Munroe. Munroe asked if you were to enquire of people where the wealthiest place on earth is located, what would they say? The diamond mines of Africa? The gold mines in South America? Or perhaps the oil fields of the Middle East? Rejecting the obvious answers, Munroe instead declared, "The wealthiest place on earth is the grave. The grave is where there is buried treasure more valuable than all the diamonds, gold and rubies of the world. In the grave, a person's potential lies buried. It holds within its grip dreams and goals that were never acted on, ideas that were never written down, thoughts that were never spoken of, and music that never came to life.

When someone dies, what mighty things could God have performed through this person if only he had been willing to stretch a little, to come out of his comfort zone and experience new growth? Some people die without ever realizing their gifts and talents; because of fear, procrastination, self doubt and various other reasons. Many people fight the calling to step out of their comfort zone, to realize and manifest their gift to the world. Some of us have been going through the motions, never realizing or finding our purpose in life—never discovering what God really wants for us.

Jack thought about this because he himself had ambitions and goals about which he often dreamed. He had nurtured these plans in his mind for most of his adult life... yet he never acted on them. He always thought he could try something new when he had more time, or when he was a little older. Maybe when he retired, or when the kids were gone. He knew that God had a destiny for him that was set in place before he was born.

> "For I know the plans I have for you," declares the Lord, "plans to prosper you and not to harm you, plans to give you hope and a future," (cf. Jer. 29:11 NIV).

Deep down Jack knew if he didn't act now, he probably never would.

Ask yourself these questions: Have you done all that you can do? Are you becoming everything you can be? What ideas and dreams have you had, but never did anything with because you allowed fear and doubt to creep in? If you were to die today, what is it that will die with you that those around you could have benefited from? Are you telling yourself that you are waiting on God? Perhaps God is waiting on you.

It goes against our true nature and against our creator just to coast through life not living up to our full potential in Christ. He expects more out of us than that. Because he loves us, God will not force us to do anything we don't want to, it's entirely up to us to step out on faith, he will provide the opportunities, but we have to seize them. He is looking for people who can set their fears aside and step out into the light. Through our achievements, his work can be accomplished. Christ can do very little by working through a defeated, fearful, insecure and spiritually immature person.

We were not created to be on the outside looking in. We are not here just to be content and comfortable with our place in life. No, we should strive to learn, to achieve and to be better every single day than we were the day before, all the while giving the thanks and glory to God who resides within us. To stop growing and learning is to stifle God's desire for us. By being content and comfortable with where we're at in life is to limit his ability to work through us.

Jesus taught multitudes with stories that held a greater message and meaning. Among the many parables Jesus shared was the following story known as the parable of the talents.

Again, it will be like a man going on a journey, who called his servants and entrusted his property to them. To one he gave five talents of money, to another two talents, and to another one talent, each according to his ability. Then he went on his journey. The man who had received the five talents went at once and put his money to work and gained five more. So also, the one with the two talents gained two more. But the man who had received the one talent went off, dug a hole in the ground and hid his master's money. "After a long time the master of those servants returned and settled accounts with them. The man who had received the five talents brought the other five. 'Master,' he said, 'you entrusted me with five talents. See, I have gained five more.' "His master replied, 'Well done, good and faithful servant! You have been faithful with a few things; I will put you in charge of many things. Come and share your master's happiness!' "The man with the two talents also came. 'Master,' he said, 'you entrusted me with two talents; see, I have gained two more.' "His master replied, 'Well done, good and faithful servant! You have been faithful with a few things; I will put you in charge of many things. Come and share your master's happiness!' "Then the man who had received the one talent came. 'Master,' he said, 'I knew that you are a hard man, harvesting where you have not sown and gathering where you have not scattered seed. So I was afraid and went out and hid your talent in the ground. See, here is what belongs to you.' "His master replied, 'You wicked, lazy servant! So you knew that I harvest where I have not sown and gather where I have not scattered seed? Well then, you should have put my money on deposit with the bankers, so that when I returned I would have received it back with interest.'" 'Take the talent from him and give it to the one who has the ten talents. For everyone who has will be given more, and he will have an abundance. Whoever does not have, even what he has will be taken from him. And throw that worthless servant outside, into the darkness, where there will be weeping and gnashing of teeth, (cf. Matt. 25:14-30 NIV).

So, what are you going to do with your talents? Whatever dreams, goals, desires and ambitions you have, they are there for a reason. Whatever you do with them is totally your choice. If you choose to bury your talents by dying with your hopes, dreams and aspirations unfulfilled, then you are free to do so. However, you as a child of God are meant to thrive.

To live out our purpose in life will have a positive and profound effect on us and everyone around us. Sometimes it could even be something that impacts the world. Even if God does not call you to change the entire world, there is still no reason that you can't change your world!

While stepping out of your comfort zone and striving to fulfill your dream, keep in mind, that it's all for the glory of him who does the work through you. Leaving your comfort zone will require hard work and persistence on your part. The enemy will try to attack you at every turn. Satan will tell you you're not good enough, smart enough, or worthy to fulfill your destiny in life. When you get on an airplane, one of the first things you must do before taking off is put on your safety belt, because on the way up you're going to experience some turbulence and resistance. It's this way in life as well. You have to fasten your, spiritual, mental and emotional safety belt as you ascend drawing closer to your dreams and goals. Eventually you will reach an altitude or a place of calm where there is strength and maturity that will enable you to overcome any obstacle the enemy places in your path.

You will receive many blessings such as joy, happiness, good health, long life, friends, financial peace and peace of mind! Just remember, that these are all to be used to bless other people and to show them the way to him. "The thief comes only to steal and kill and destroy; I have come that they may have life, and have it to the full," (*cf.* John 10:10 NIV).

Just like in the parable that Jesus spoke of in Matthew, we have all been given talents by our master. It is entirely up to us to do something with them. When we stand before God one day, he may ask what we did with our talents. Let's decide today to do everything we can to multiply them many times; so someday our master can say to us, "Well done my good and faithful servant."

You have talents and you have greatness within you because you were created in the image of God. Ask him to guide you, to show you your gifts. Ask him for wisdom as James encourages us, "If any of you lacks wisdom, let him ask of God, who gives to all liberally and without reproach, and it will be given to him," (*cf.* James 1:5 NKJV).

As wisdom begins to dwell with you and in you, the Holy Spirit will give you a passion, a desire, a dream about doing certain things with your life. When you have these thoughts, it's what you do with them that matters most. Write your thoughts down on paper, act on them, plan a course of action that aligns with your dreams and aspirations and be willing to step out in faith and fulfill them.

Work on yourself daily and improve day-to-day and moment-to-moment, so that you will be an example to others. Your improvement comes through prayer, studying the word of God and by fellowship with other believers. Also practice the art of taking your thoughts captive and making them obedient to the will of Christ, always be aware of the words you speak.

When we put bits into the mouths of horses to make them obey us, we can turn the whole animal. Or take ships as an example. Although they are so large and are driven by strong winds, they are steered by a very small rudder wherever the pilot wants to go. Likewise the tongue is a small part of the body, but it makes great boasts. Consider what a great forest is set on fire by a small spark, (*cf.* James 3:3-5 NIV).

Improving daily requires some effort on your part, but through practice and persistence you can develop yourself to the point these things become habit. You cannot go through life with one foot in and one foot out. This will not get you where you want to go, don't focus on the times you fail. Because there will be times every day that you fall short and miss the mark, just get back up and keep moving forward.

Surely goodness and mercy shall follow me all the days of my life; and I will dwell in the house of the Lord forever, (*cf.* Psalm 23:6 NKJV).

2
❧Self Mastery❧

In the course of time
Cain brought some of the fruits of the soil
as an offering to the Lord.
But Abel brought fat portions
from some of the firstborn of his flock.
The Lord looked with favor on Abel and his offering,
but on Cain and his offering he did not look with favor.
So Cain was very angry, and his face was downcast.
Then the Lord said to Cain,
"Why are you angry? Why is your face downcast?
If you do what is right, will you not be accepted?
But if you do not do what is right,
sin is crouching at your door;
it desires to have you, but you must master it."

Genesis 4:3-7 NIV

The seventh verse of Genesis chapter four talks about mastering sin. Cain was struggling with jealousy, anger and revenge after his offering to God was rejected. God told Cain he must master sin, which is the same as mastering himself. Cain was showing weakness spiritually, mentally and emotionally. If we are to become the men and women God wants us to be; if we are to continue reaching new levels and new potentials in our life—then we must master ourselves to the best of our abilities. We were created by God in his image, in his likeness (*cf.* Gen. 1:27). We are here to glorify him. One way we can do this by always moving ahead, always expanding and stepping out of our comfort zone. Become active in church as a greeter, an usher, or helping to clean. Churches are always in need of help in one way or another. Ask your church how you can be of help; ask where you are needed then be open to pitch in wherever there is a space to fill. Look for volunteer organizations or nonprofit groups in your community and get involved. Toastmasters is an excellent place to develop speaking and listening skills, both of which will make you more confident in every situation you encounter. These are all areas that can take us out of our comfort zone and spark new growth spiritually, mentally and emotionally. As we do this we develop discipline and character, we grow in maturity through God and his word. The result of this growth is self-mastery by way of obedience.

> Then the Lord said to Cain, "Where is your brother Abel?" "I don't know," he replied. "Am I my brother's keeper? The Lord said, "What have you done? Listen! Your brother's blood cries out to me from the ground. Now you are under a curse and driven from the ground, which opened its mouth to receive your brother's blood from your hand. When you work the ground, it will no longer yield its crops for you. You will be a restless wanderer on the earth." Cain said to the Lord, "My punishment is more than I can bear. Today you are driving me from the land, and I will be hidden from your presence; I will be a restless wanderer on the earth, and whoever finds me will kill me," (cf. Gen. 4:9-14 NIV).

As you read the conversation between God and Cain, it's clear that Cain never showed any remorse whatsoever. He was neither sorry nor did he ask for God's forgiveness. God knew Cain had killed his brother and when he asked him about it the first thing Cain did was to answer not only with a lie, but also with a bad attitude. In modern language he is saying "How should I know where my brother is, I'm not his babysitter!" Then even after the Lord tells Cain what his punishment will be, Cain still shows no remorse. He is only concerned about himself. He begins to complain to God about how bad his punishment is and how it's too much. He said to God, "It's more than I can bear." Cain's only concerns are with "I" and "me." Cain has a problem with the way he thinks; he lacks the maturity to control his emotions. He cares only about himself and no one else. When we read the entire story of Cain and Abel it is obvious that Cain struggles with issues not much different from those we face today. Most people who are stable and achieve a certain level of spiritual, mental and emotional maturity have the ability to recognize when things start going south, then turn to God for guidance. When we do something we know we shouldn't, or when we catch ourselves doing something wrong, we simply try harder to do better next time. If Cain was capable of having this type of bad behavior after he has already been confronted by God, then what was he like before this happened?

When we bring our offerings to God we are told in Proverbs 3:9-10 to give the first fruits. In this day and age many of us tithe (*cf.* Heb. 7:7-8, 1 Cor. 16:1-3) which means to give ten percent. In the Old Testament days, they would bring their best and offer it up to God as an offering or a sacrifice. Genesis 4:4 says that Abel brought from the first born, [the first fruits]. So, it stands to reason that with Cain's bad attitude he most likely did not bring God his best or his first fruits. He only brought what he wanted and on top of that, he gave it grudgingly. He was not what we would call "a cheerful giver," nor was he coming from a place of love. After God rejected Cain's gift, Cain became angry and it showed on his face. This is where God said to him something very amazing; something that is a warning not just to Cain, but to all of us. God knew that Cain was headed for serious trouble if he didn't get his thoughts and emotions under control.

God said to Cain, in Genesis 4:6-7 (NIV), "Why are you angry? Why is your face downcast? If you do what is right, will you not be accepted? But if you do not do what is right, sin is crouching at your door; it desires to have you, but you must master it."

I believe God was telling Cain that he must master not just sin, but he must master himself. Cain was not following after his spirit; he was walking after his flesh. His spirit was weak, which in turn caused him to be weak mentally. He did not take captive the thoughts in his mind. These thoughts manifest themselves emotionally through anger, jealousy and a feeling of rejection. Then Cain's mental and emotional weaknesses get out of hand and the results are physical violence and the death of his brother.

There is a serious lesson here to be learned: in order for us to live the life God wants for us, to be the men and women God wants us to be, we must master our habits and our life because sin is daily crouching at our door. It seeks to overtake us in a moment of weakness.

For us to reach our full potential in Christ and to fulfill the destiny God has for us in this brief life, we have to master sin by mastering ourselves. Taking captive our thoughts and the renewing of our mind is not something we can do on a daily basis, it must be done moment-to-moment. The things you do are never more important at any time than they are in this very moment.

When thoughts enter our mind and we speak words that reflect those thoughts, it activates the spiritual realm in either one of two ways. It will either be good or evil; positive or negative, (*cf.* Matt. 12:34-37). When thoughts creep in we first have to practice recognizing them, then take them captive and make them obedient to Christ. Because Cain was weak spiritually, mentally and emotionally, his thoughts and his mind overtook him. He became trapped in his mind; he had this story in his head of being inadequate, feelings of rejection and anger crept in. His *ego* was controlling his entire life at this point. He then had the thought of murder and used his words to entice Abel into a field where he killed him.

Self-mastery is when we bring our life into the obedience of Christ. It is to consistently strive to be in the presence of God and to study his word to the point that we are better equipped to take captive our thoughts. We are to strengthen ourselves spiritually, mentally and emotionally so we will be better able to overcome the temptation to sin and thus allow God to work through us.

God can work through you and I, he can use us no matter where we are in life. But the more we master ourselves and the more we master the way we live in this life, the better able he will be to accomplish great things through us. As Christians, it is important for us to take care of our half of the whole. As we grow in our knowledge of God and his word, we also grow in maturity in every area of our life. Feeding his word and positive messages into our mind is the beginning to our growth and expansion. And not just *reading* his words, but obeying his words.

We are all flawed. We all fall short of the glory of God every day. However, when we begin to live as God wants we will grow and mature. We will set foot down the road to self-mastery, which in turn will provide us the discipline and maturity to master sin and to resist temptation when they rear their ugly heads. The key is to focus our thoughts and mind on the things of God and Christ. Paul tells us, "Finally, brothers, whatever is true, whatever is noble, whatever is right, whatever is pure, whatever is lovely, whatever is admirable—if anything is excellent or praiseworthy—think about such things," (*cf.* Phil. 4:8 NIV). As we do this we will mature and become strong in spirit, mind and body.

To be spiritually, mentally, emotionally, physically, socially and financially secure is what we as parents desire for our children. If we as flawed humans love our children and want success for them in every area of their life – then how much more does God, who is perfect in every way, want the best for us?

Jesus tells us to ask, to seek and to knock and assures us that everyone who asks, receives. Everyone who knocks, the door will be opened. Perhaps you need a raise in pay, a better job, a spouse? On the other hand, maybe you want the Lord to show you your purpose in life and to guide you into the plan he has for you. What are you doing about it? It's not all about you, but you are half of the equation. You can pray all you want, but until you begin to improve yourself and walk in obedience, God will not help you. We read in Matthew 19:26, "With God all things are possible." However if you are struggling with porn, drugs, or alcoholism God will not bless certain parts of your life because you are not positioning yourself to receive the blessings he has waiting for you. I was told about a man once who had been married and divorced several times. He really wanted a good marriage and a family but he stayed out all night drinking and doing drugs. God was having a difficult time blessing him with a loving peaceful home because he was engaged in activities that were blocking the blessing. Self-improvement includes every area of your life; spiritual, mental, emotional, physical, social and financial. Developing discipline and maturity in every area of your life is to improve who you are as a person. What is blocking the blessings in your life? What areas do you need to improve?

To improve one-self is to change the way you think, to change your vocabulary; this in turn changes the way you act and come across to others. For whatever is in a man's heart so he is. Whatever we think about and whatever we feed into our mind has a profound effect on the way we talk, this has an impact on how we act and how we are received. Our happiness, facial expressions and body language are all a reflection of how we feel on the inside. Reading hundreds of books or camping out in front of the computer is not the answer. Reading and learning are all good, but only to a certain extent. At some point, we have to put into practice the knowledge that we are receiving. Start working, today, right now on improving yourself. In every area of your life, work on self-mastery. God will open your eyes so when you seek you will find, when you prayerfully ask you will receive and when you knock, doors will open that were once closed. He will make a way where there was no way.

Cain's destiny was in his hands. God warned him and told him what he must do. Cain had the ability to bring heaven or hell on earth into his life. He was unable to master himself therefore he had no ability to master the sin that was overtaking him. You and I need to learn from his mistake and take the necessary steps to bring our self to a place where we can let go of the fears in this life, fear of rejection, feelings of inadequacy and insecurity.

Once we do this, God will make us "attractive," so to speak. Through him we will attract the things in life that we need. We will have no reason to want, nor will we suffer any form of lack. Some have taught that Jesus was a poor man; others have taught that he was wealthy. Both sides are missing the point of his life. Jesus was teaching by example to lean on God. He was showing us that if we do our part he will do his. Jesus never wanted for anything, nor did he lack anything he needed. Jesus mastered himself, his mind and emotions by overcoming his flesh and because of this he mastered sin. That is what God was telling Cain to do. This is what he wants from us.

You have talents inside of you that were put into place by the Lord himself. He blessed you with gifts, talents and a divine purpose for your life. Do not go to the grave without striving and giving all you have to reach the full potential God gave you. Give God more to work with by developing your talents and developing yourself through self-mastery.

IF YOU READ HISTORY YOU WILL
FIND THAT THE CHRISTIANS WHO
DID MOST FOR THE PRESENT WORLD
WERE PRECISELY THOSE WHO
THOUGHT MOST OF THE NEXT.
IT IS SINCE CHRISTIANS HAVE LARGELY
CEASED TO THINK OF THE OTHER
WORLD THAT THEY HAVE BECOME SO
INEFFECTIVE IN THIS

—C.S. Lewis

3
⊰Seek God First⊱

I can do all things through Christ
who strengthens men.

Philippians 4:13 NKJV

Seeking God is the beginning to everything. Your potential, purpose in life, happiness and everything required to have an abundant life will manifest itself not by being religious, not by following different laws that men have established, but simply by first seeking the kingdom of God in everything you do, (*cf.* Matt. 6:33). We are joint heirs with Abraham and it is not through doctrines and laws that we receive the promise, but by faith (*cf.* Rom. 4). Making him Lord and savior of your life, having faith and a deep desire to obey his commands will be the beginning to the changes in your new life.

We on our own can accomplish very little in the way of happiness and peace of mind. True peace of mind, happiness and our life purpose will manifest itself when we learn to become whole; being whole means to be well balanced. As we start working on becoming a whole, complete person, we will see amazing things happening in our life. God will begin to transform us: we will become new. It is written in Revelation 21:5b, (NKJV) "Behold, I make all things new," and that includes us! He will put new people and relationships in our life. People will begin to cross our path that will help us along our way: they will help us to grow and we will learn from each other. Because God has made each of us unique, endowing each of us with our very own set of gifts and talents, we each have something to offer. Through fellowship with one another, God will strengthen us, add to our knowledge and skills, fill in gaps in our understanding and bring us towards wholeness. Becoming a well-balanced person all starts with God and his word. As scripture grips us, balance will be a continuous journey of growth and life that never ends.

In order to begin the journey of becoming a whole person, becoming the man or woman God wants us to be, there are six areas of our life that need to be developed: Spiritual, Mental, Emotional, Physical, Social and Financial

The emotional aspect is actually a subcategory of Mental, but I have chosen to list it on its own because our emotions are so powerful that they warrant their own category. Some people say we should be complete in mind, body and spirit, but this is totally backwards and in the wrong order. It should be spirit first, then mind/emotions and finally body. To grow spiritually is to grow in every area of our life.

In Greek, there is the word *sozo*, which is translated into English as salvation. *Sozo*—or salvation—means to heal and to make whole. It represents the blessings on us from Christ. Our salvation, our *sozo*, is for the whole man and woman, spiritually, mentally, emotionally and physically. This is not only for the afterlife but also for the here and now.

Spiritual is at the top of the list because we cannot be whole and balanced without a personal relationship with Jesus. In order to enjoy a personal relationship with Christ we must take care of our half of the whole: pray confessing our sins, seek his forgiveness, not lean on our own understanding but trust in Christ to meet our daily needs. We can't do his job only God can do that. He will not force us to do our job. He will always hold up his end, but because he loves us, he gave us free will. We have the power to make up our own minds and to make our own decisions. Therefore, we have to take care of our half of the whole by keeping these six areas strong. If we are lacking or suffering in any one or two of these six areas, it will create imbalance and almost always drag the others down.

To live the life that God has in store for us; to live out our full potential and use the talents our master gave us before we were even conceived, developing our spiritual life is a must. Once again, this doesn't mean becoming *religious* just showing up at church on Sunday, having the fish emblem on your car, or having the old family Bible sitting on the coffee table. It means to simply seek God, to defeat your flesh and be led by the spirit. It means to lose your ego—to lose yourself and to realize that it's not about you. You're involved, obviously, but your involvement is to allow him to get you to a place where he can work through you, a place where you can serve. "If a man cleanses himself from the latter, he will be an instrument for noble purposes, made holy, useful to the Master and prepared to do any good work," (*cf.* 2 Tim. 2:21 NIV).

This world is in dire need of Christ followers who can step up as leaders; but a good leader is the person who knows how to serve. You will become a leader by being a servant. Then He said to His disciples, "The harvest truly is plentiful, but the laborers are few. Therefore pray the Lord of the harvest to send out laborers into His harvest," (*cf.* Matt. 9:37-38 NKJV). God can use you now wherever you happen to be, but that doesn't mean that where you are now is where you're going to stay. As you move out of your comfort zone and mature spiritually, He will be able to use you in greater ways.

The greatest changes in life will come when we develop the discipline to allow our spirit to lead our flesh. Even though we live in a three-dimensional body we will be operating in the fourth dimension [spiritual realm] when we do live in this discipline. The battle between our flesh and our spirit is fought and won moment to moment on a daily basis. Since we live by the spirit, let us keep in step with the spirit (*cf.* Gal. 5:25).

Even Jesus had to overcome his flesh in order that we might be saved. "Going a little farther, he fell with his face to the ground and prayed, 'My Father, if it is possible, may this cup be taken from me. Yet not as I will, but as you will,'" (*cf.* Matt. 26:39 NIV). His flesh wanted to find an easier way, to allow what was about to come, to pass away, but his spirit ruled when he said "Yet not as I will, but as you will."

We must at all times safeguard our spiritual lives and keep Christ at the forefront. Keeping God as our main priority in life and doing what he wants is the only way to have true peace, prosperity and happiness in our life. How do we know what God wants? By reading his word, meditating on it and praying daily. Even if it's only twenty to thirty minutes a day, make it a priority to set aside time to pray and to read and meditate on the scripture. For me, early mornings are my favorite time and also at night in bed. Beginning the day and ending the day with his word will help you to discover who he is and what he wants. Draw closer to him and he will draw closer to you. As time goes by you'll begin to hear that still small voice guiding and directing your every step. When we read the Bible, it tells us about God and how we are to live as Christ followers. Paul tells us in 2 Timothy 3:16-17, "All Scripture is God-breathed and is useful for teaching, rebuking, correcting and training in righteousness, so that the servant of God may be thoroughly equipped for every good work." In everything you do, and every where you go seek God. In the words of A.W. Tozer "God formed us for His pleasure, [Revelation 4;11] and so formed us that we, as well as He, can, in divine communion, enjoy the sweet and mysterious mingling of kindred personalities. He meant us to see Him and live with Him and draw our life from His smile.

4

❧Identity❧

I have been crucified with Christ
and I no longer live, but Christ lives in me.
The life I live in the body,
I live by faith in the Son of God,
who loved me and gave himself for me,

Galatians 2:20 NIV

A foundational way to develop ourselves spiritually and mature into our new lives as Christians, to reach our full potential, is to know where we came from and who we are. So many of us identify ourselves with our parents and our family members; we make up excuses for our weaknesses by blaming them. We say, "Well my daddy had a bad temper so I guess I got it from him." "My mamma smoked cigarettes her entire life so I guess that's why I do too." Perhaps we've heard something like this, "My dad died of a heart attack at age 50 and I probably will as well." "My uncle was addicted to pornography, so I learned that from him." Here is an attempt to justify, "I was abused by a relative, so now I'm abusive towards others."

The list of such is nearly endless. When we are born again through Christ we receive a new identity, (*cf.* 2 Cor. 5:17). We didn't come from our parents, we came from God. He simply used them as a vehicle to get us here. Just because our parents, grandparents, siblings, or whomever may have had many flaws and didn't know how to deal with them, is no excuse for us to live the same way. We have a new identity in Christ. To blame our family for the way we are is simply a way to justify how we act and live. It's always easier to blame someone else, remain the way we are and continue to wallow in our problems and live a defeated life. It's also lazy, because it takes work to change who you are. Nobody can change you. You must do it yourself; change has to come from within. If you don't want to change, then nobody else can make you. Neither will God. He will provide the avenues and opportunities for you, but He'll never force you to change.

There are those that teach we should just accept who we are; that we should embrace ourselves with our meager abilities and manifold shortcomings. Adopting that logic, you'll never grow beyond where you're at right now. However, as we mature spiritually and mentally change has to be inevitable. To mature is to change; we are to put off the old person and put on the new (*cf.* Eph. 4:22-24). We are new creatures in Christ and we have a new identity (*cf.* 2 Cor. 5:17). To embrace our position in life, who we are right now, is to stop growing. It means we will go to the grave and our talents will be forever buried with us. You have great potential within you, but change is essential if you want to continue realizing your potential. To accept who you are and where you're at in life is to conclude that you have no more to offer; that you have already grown all you can grow and that you have learned all you'll ever be able to know. Spiritual growth however never ceases; growth comes moment-to-moment and day-to-day. This growth continues every day until we are dead. And we should strive to die with nothing left, meaning that we gave all we had, that we stepped out of our comfort zone and expanded our spirit and mind till we could feel the stretch marks on our life. Let us die knowing we used to the utmost the talents our master gave us, anything less than this is a tragedy, and in my opinion...a sin.

I believe God wants and expects, more out of us than to stand idle while the gifts he blessed us with go to waste. To develop a strong spiritual life is to stay in the word and daily seek the Lord. Do not look to another man or woman for your deliverance or as your source of happiness. Make sure that what you are being taught is Biblically sound. If you allow your happiness and needs to be met spiritually by a man or woman you'll be let down sooner or later, one day causing you to possibly question everything you've ever been taught. We all make mistakes, even our leaders.

God wants us to have a close relationship with him and with each other. The Bible says that God will be glad and that he will calm us with his love and He will rejoice over us with singing.

> The Lord your God in your midst,
> The Mighty One, will save;
> He will rejoice over you with gladness,
> He will quiet you with His love,
> He will rejoice over you with singing.
>
> Zephaniah 3:17 (NKJV)

I had the opportunity to listen to Andrew Wommack speak in Durant, Oklahoma. He mentioned that in the Garden of Eden Adam and Eve only saw with their spiritual eyes. They were naked and felt no shame. They had the tree of the knowledge of good and evil in the middle of the Garden, yet they paid it no attention. After they partook of the fruit, the Bible tells us in Genesis 3:7 that their eyes were opened and they saw that they were naked. They now were seeing in the carnal; before this, they lived by faith and only saw with their spiritual eyes. We as Christians have the ability, by faith, to operate in the spiritual realm.

Most people focus on their past, where they came from and on the opinions of others. You may see no way to rise above your current situation and become more successful in life; but that is the carnal way of thinking. To live and operate in the spirit is to pay no attention to what you think, see, feel, or hear in the flesh, but to walk in the faith of what you know based on the word of God. You should look for and expect supernatural things to happen in your life daily. However, we get so focused on our problems and the things of this world, that we miss God; we are so focused on "stuff" that we rarely see him. Then, when we get in a bind or go through some dramatic event in our life we wonder why he is not there. God is always there we just have to be available. We have to allow ourselves to be present so that he can reveal himself to us. He never leaves us. The scripture Hebrews 13:5 tells us know the Lord will never leave us nor forsake us; it's our mind that leaves him. If we can have the presence of mind to open our spiritual eyes, we will sense his presence.

Imagine you're out in the wilderness on a camping trip. It's a cold dark night and you have a big fire. Imagine what it's like as you move close to it, then farther away from it. When you stand next to the fire there is warmth; you are standing in the light of the fire so you are able to see things that you couldn't see before; you feel safe and confident in the light and warmth of this fire. But as you move away from the fire it begins to get colder, your vision starts to go away and you eventually lose your ability to see clearly because you are now standing in darkness. The fire never moves; it's constant. You are the one moving in and out of the light. That's how we treat God. He is always there. He is the same yesterday, today and forever (*cf.* Heb. 13:8), he is always here with us (*cf.* Matt. 28:20); but the decisions we make in life, the words we speak and the actions we perform, will cause us to move in and out of God's presence. It's not God who moves away from us...it's you and I who move away from God.

To continually remain in God's presence by staying in the scriptures, by praying without ceasing and always being conscious, is to be made new in the attitude of your minds (*cf.* Eph. 4:23). This allows our minds to gradually over time become renewed and the renewing never stops. "Do not conform any longer to the pattern of this world, but be transformed by the renewing of your mind. Then you will be able to test and approve what God's will is—his good, pleasing and perfect will," (cf. Rom. 12:2 NIV).

When the Bible talks about the renewing of our minds, that's not something we do once and then forget it. We need to renew our minds daily through prayer, reading and meditating on God's word and through fellowship with other believers so that we can stay in the light and warmth of his love and mercy.

We are to pray without ceasing, which means to talk with him all the time, in everything we do. A prayer isn't just about asking God for things; prayer is about fellowship with him and fellowship should be seen as an intimate relationship. If your children only talked to you when they wanted something, when they only wanted money or some other favor, how would you feel? How do you feel when they don't want anything except just to talk and spend some time with you, just to check in and tell you about their day? How would you feel if your small child or grandchild crawled up in your lap and looked up at you and said, "I just want to sit with you for a while because you're the best and I love you"?

Praying, talking and enjoying intimate fellowship with God is not about asking him for things. Sometimes it's just about talking and sharing: sometimes it's about being personal and intimate with him. You don't have to drop to your knees or go into a closet; wherever you happen to be simply speak with him in your mind. Thank him for another day of life and health, for that good grade your child received or for that little something that made you smile. Throughout the day practice sharing with him until it becomes a habit; and you'll find that your relationship with him will start to change and become stronger.

Psalm 46:10 reads, "Be still and know that I am God." Every so often practice being still and realize that sometimes you don't need to talk; sometimes all you need to do is sit in his lap and just "be." It's during these times that you'll be able to hear him whispering to your heart.

Calling ourselves Christian is one thing, living for God is another. So many of us today believe in God; we believe that Jesus died for our sins, but that's where it stops. For some of us it just hasn't become real yet. It's as though Christians are walking around with blinders on. Most of us believe in a heaven and hell in the after-life, but what so many of us don't realize is that we have access to heaven and hell now. Heaven and hell are both right here with us.

Once, having been asked by the Pharisees when the kingdom of God would come, Jesus replied, "The kingdom of God does not come with your careful observation, nor will people say, 'Here it is,' or 'There it is,' because the kingdom of God is within you," (*cf.* Luke 17:20b-21 NIV).

There are millions of people all over the world that are living a life that is dead. Their life is nothing but a space in time, just waiting to die, to leave this world so they can live in heaven with peace, joy, happiness, abundance, love and so many other things that seem out of reach to them now. God doesn't want us to wait until we die to experience these things; they are available right here, right now!

But the fruit of the Spirit is love, joy, peace, patience, kindness, goodness, faithfulness, gentleness and self-control. Against such things there is no law, (*cf.* Gal. 5:22-23 NIV).

Spending time worrying about paying the bills and how you are going to make ends meet can be a thing of the past when you get your spiritual life in order. To worry about what's going to happen is to fear. When we worry about money, clothes, bills and other things that we need, it is the same as being fearful. Worry is a fear-based emotion. That doesn't mean that we shouldn't take the proper steps to guard our health and our finances; to ignore a dangerous situation is wrong. However, excessive worry and fear is also wrong as well as unhealthy.

Jesus when speaking to his disciples would often teach them with parables. In the parable below, Jesus address's the topic of worry; which is a manifestation of fear.

Then Jesus said to his disciples: 'Therefore I tell you, do not worry about your life, what you will eat; or about your body, what you will wear. Life is more than food and the body more than clothes. Consider the ravens: They do not sow or reap, they have no storeroom or barn; yet God feeds them. And how much more valuable you are than birds! Who of you by worrying can add a single hour to his life? Since you cannot do this very little thing, why do you worry about the rest, (cf. Matt. 6:25-34, Luke 12:22-26 NIV).

Just think about it: what would it be like not to worry or have fear in your life? Without these things, what's left? Peace of mind, happiness and joy are what's left. They are yours for the taking by making God a real part of your life. Don't be confused about how you will make ends meet, because God is not the author of confusion (cf. 1 Cor. 14:33). Don't be fearful of what tomorrow will bring because God did not create us to have a spirit of fear (cf. 2 Tim. 1:7). Lean on him, stay in prayer and pursue God with everything you have. The Lord our God will make a way where there was no way. A certain amount of fear and worry happens to all of us. Just get into the word and surround yourself with wise, Godly people, become part of a body, find a good church, pray, meditate and read books by Christian authors. Do these things until you're strong enough spiritually to step out and help others who are struggling with their life and their beliefs. We are taught that Jesus will return one day; that there will be a great rapture. In a sense, there are people who are being raptured now! Every single day people are being caught up and leaving their old life behind.

But there are also many Christians today who are living in the past and looking to the future. Why not live in the moment and take care of what needs to be taken care of now? There is work to be done right here, right now! We read about past events, how God was doing great works in ancient, Biblical times. Then we look to the future for Jesus to rapture us because we want to escape the work he has for us here and now. To me, that's just plain lazy and its immoral for us to think that way. God is doing great things now, just the same as he was 2000 years ago. People today are being set free from sickness and disease, from addictions and corrupt lifestyles; just as they were in the days Jesus walked the Earth as a man.

For us to spend all of our time worrying about the rapture and thinking about ourselves and what we want, is the same as worrying about tomorrow. Jesus said not to worry about tomorrow, tomorrow can worry for itself. We have enough trouble taking care of today. "Therefore do not worry about tomorrow, for tomorrow will worry about itself. Each day has enough trouble of its own," (*cf.* Matt. 6:34 NIV).

If we live today the way we're supposed to live and do God's work for him now, then we don't have to worry about tomorrow. By being the men and women we're supposed to be now, tomorrow will take care of itself.

The word rapture comes from the Greek word *Harpazo*, which means to get "caught up" or "snatched." Let's get caught up and snatched now! We can in a sense be raptured now; we should allow our flesh and ego to die and by doing that we'll be caught up with Christ now, living and being led by the spirit. I'm not saying that things like the rapture or the second coming of Christ are irrelevant, what I'm saying is that we don't have to worry about what the master is going to do in the future if we're doing what he wants us to do now.

Dr. Cho is an amazing pastor who lives in South Korea. He currently has the largest church in the world. When he was trying to build his church in Korea, he ran into an obstacle trying to get the Koreans to believe in the God of the Bible. Dr. Cho recalls that when he would talk to the people they wanted to know where God lived. The Buddha they worshipped had a house, a physical place and an address where he stayed, so they always knew where to find him when they wanted to worship him. So naturally, when they started hearing about the God the Christians worship, they wanted to know where he lived so they could go and see him. Cho thought about this and sought a solution to this dilemma. He had a deep desire to tell the Korean people where they could find God. Dr. Cho decided that he would ask, "God where are you? Are you there? Here? Where? Please give me your address." So, he prayed and believed that God would give him the answer. Finally, the Holy Spirit told Dr. Cho what to tell the Koreans. So when they asked where God lived Cho told them: "We can find the location of God. I have now found his address. His address is my address, and he dwelleth in me with all power and authority. Through the Holy Spirit God the Father and God the Son dwelleth in me, and he goes with me where I go.

> He also dwells within you, and his address is your address. If you stay in your home, he is there; if you go to your place of business, he is there; if you work in the kitchen, he is there. God dwelleth within you, and his resources are found in you.*

> At that day you will know that I am in My Father, and you in Me, and I in you, (*cf.* John 14:20 NKJV).

Dr. Cho was right on the mark. God has a home; he has a place where he lives. Have you ever wondered where God resides? You can see it if you want, it's as simple as looking

*[Source: "The Fourth Dimension" By Dr. Paul Yonggi Cho]

in the mirror—he lives inside of you! Therefore, greatness is within you and there is nothing you can't achieve with God in the lead. He has already blessed you with talents and potential, but it's up to you to discover and cultivate those talents. Stretch yourself, step out of your comfort zone and expand your spirit and mind until you feel the stretch marks on your entire life.

If you've accepted Jesus as your Lord and Savior and sought his forgiveness for all your sins, then all of your sins have been forgiven; they are removed from you as far as the east is from the west. You are made brand new; you have a new identity in Christ. There is no limit to the things he has in store for you in this life.

5
◈Our Mind◈

Do not be anxious about anything,
but in everything, by prayer and petition,
with thanksgiving,
present your requests to God.
And the peace of God,
which transcends all understanding,
will guard your hearts and your minds in Christ Jesus.

Philippians 4:6-7 NIV

Our state of mind is very important. Just as we have to develop ourselves spiritually, we also have to develop ourselves mentally by constantly renewing our minds. The renewing of your mind takes place daily when reading the word, praying, worshipping and through fellowship with other Christians. When we practice these things, our mind stays renewed, keeping us from being conformed to the world. It's a daily battle dying to self, trying to keep our egos in subjection. We take care of our cars and house. We spend a fortune on health clubs and health food trying to take care of our bodies. These things are all fine and dandy, but why do we often overlook the one thing we can least afford to lose...our minds?

As you become more aware of your thoughts and their effect on your life, it's obvious the main difference between the people who have the fruit of the spirit and the people who do not [people who achieve abundant life versus those who do not] has to do with the way they think. Do you often allow others to control how you think and feel?

When we allow others to make us mad, depressed, worried, or cause us to feel negative emotions as a result of something they may have said or done, or when we blame all of our problems on other people, then we are allowing them to control our lives.

As Christians nobody owes us anything; we rely on God and when possible on each other. God does not just suddenly hand over anything; we have to do the work. God accomplished some great things through Moses, but Moses had to do some of the work. Moses had to strengthen his mind and then his faith in order to carry out God's will. When Moses had problems, when the people began to murmur [just imagine 2 million people complaining] he didn't start blaming everybody in sight; he went to God and in return God sent men like Aaron and Jethro. God, through Jethro, laid it out for Moses exactly how to delegate responsibility and make life a little easier. God also used Aaron to be there for Moses, to help him with his mission and to carry out the commands of God. He will do the same thing for us as we begin to renew our minds. God will put people in our lives that will help us to grow!

The sooner we realize that God or the government or anyone else for that matter owes us nothing other than protection and the space to grow, the better off we'll be. People who have the idea that their problems are someone else's fault or that someone else is keeping them from joy and peace of mind, will never progress in life unless they change the way they think. By renewing our minds, we are basically rewiring them.

You've probably heard the phrase "Let go and let God." This expression is a loaded statement, which is over used. Yes, we should let God control our lives, but there has to be action on our part. Praying to him and wanting improvement in our lives requires work on our end. So it's all well and good to "let go and let God" as long as you realize that simply means to let him work through you; not expecting him to do all the work himself, because he will not do that. If you express to God that you want to be a nurse and ask for his help you still have to go to nursing school. If you pray and ask God for a promotion at work or to find a new job, you still have to improve yourself and your skills to qualify for that new position or that new job. What God will then do is help you to find favor in the eyes of those who can help you accomplish your goals. Your job is to do the work. He will create the opportunities and open your eyes to the right path and the right answers along the way.

As Christians, we must consider how we are viewed and received by the world. Christians have done so much harm by not walking in love, by not treating people who hold different views from ours with dignity, respect and love. We are to be examples, provoking people to ask about the joy and the hope inside of us, allowing us to share the gospel to anyone that asks. We create the way others view us and treat us; not only as Christians, but as individuals. We should always strive to approach others from a place of love. When you begin to change your mind set, then you'll begin to change the way you look at people. Popular writer Dr. Wayne Dyer is quoted as saying, "When you change the way you look at things, then the things you look at will change." This also applies to the way we look at people.

The story below testifies to how our spirit, mind and body are all connected. When one component is neglected, the others will soon follow.

Several years ago I was close to someone who began to let his health slip away. He was overworking himself and he didn't care what he ate as long as it was fast and easy. His attitude towards diet and the world in general grew progressively worse. It manifested itself in the forms of anger, self-doubt, impatience, fear and self-pity. Between his poor diet and high levels of stress, his blood pressure would sometimes climb to the point that the vessels in his nose would rupture and bleed for twenty to thirty minutes. [This concerned me because hypertension to the point of severe nosebleeds could have been an early warning sign of a stroke or heart attack.] He was very irritable and impatient with family and friends. It didn't take long for him to realize this had to stop, One day out of sheer anger and frustration, he decided that he was sick and tired of being sick and tired. This had to come to an end! He resolved to change the way his mind processed information. By doing this he would not only be happier and healthier but would also add years to his life, not to mention be a better husband and dad. He had a basic knowledge of God and knew right from wrong, but over the years, he had just been going through the motions. He realized that over the course of his life he had been doing the same things repeatedly but life was not getting any better.

Albert Einstein once said, "The definition of insanity is doing the same thing over and over again and expecting different results."

Not only did he change the way he ate, but he slowly started changing his thought process. He also added daily prayer and he began reading his Bible more. Whenever he could, he started listening to motivational speakers and reading books on positive thinking. Although he didn't realize it at the time, this was the Holy Spirit working in him. God was calling.

It has been said that in the last few minutes before you fall asleep your mind is the most receptive to new thoughts and ideas.

So, he started reading and praying at night as he lay in bed waiting to fall asleep. He kept this up for maybe a month or two. One night after he had finished reading and praying he was blessed with a dream.

In his dream, he and another man were at a lady's house helping her do some work. It was a two-story house that sat atop a hill. They were on the second floor when the woman noticed a storm approaching. A second glance revealed it to be a tornado! So the three of them ran outside into a low-wooded area and laid down in this low spot in the hopes that the tornado would pass over them. He looked up at the tornado; a huge, black, dirty, swirling mass was heading straight for him! He noticed as he laid on the ground the trunk of a medium-sized tree right in front of him, so he wrapped his arms around the base of it hoping this would keep him from being carried off. At that moment, he looked up once more in the direction of the storm and the tornado was only a few yards away, but this time it was not a big black swirling mass; it was much different, this time it was completely clear. He could actually see through it. Inside of it were arcs and electrical currents and what appeared to be long streaks of electricity flashing around. They were all spinning in a circular motion.

The only way to describe it would be as a transparent electric tornado. He could see that it was much lower than before and now the tip was dragging the ground straight for him! At that very moment, he squeezed the tree tighter and cried out for God to save him. He could feel his legs and body rise off of the ground as he clutched tightly to the tree, similar to a flag straining on a pole during a windy day. He was most certain that life was about to be over. He knew this was the end and that he was going to die. As the point of the tornado that was dragging the ground went straight across his head, it felt as though it went through him. There were electrical currents and circuits flashing in his brain. And then all at once the storm was gone. As he stood up, he could hardly believe that he was alive. And then it dawned on him; his mind wasn't the same. It had been rewired so that he would never think the same way again.

He now knew that this was a blessing from the Holy Spirit. This dream could not and should not be ignored. At first, he didn't tell anybody, but of one thing he was sure; the results were real. Over the next several months he detected definite changes in the way he thought and viewed the world. He was a new man and had become a work in progress, trying to make each day better than the one before. His desire for growth and his quality of life continue to increase to this day. He now understands that he is being sanctified, or "set apart" by God for a Holy purpose; he is daily reminded and confident from Philippians 1:6 that he who has begun a good work in you is faithful to complete it.

"Do not conform any longer to the pattern of this world, but be transformed by the renewing of your mind. Then you will be able to test and approve what God's will is—his good, pleasing and perfect will," (cf. Rom. 12:2 NIV).

When your mind is renewed by God, it is literally rewired. You now have a new identity and the way you view life will begin to change. As you are being led by your spirit rather than your flesh, you'll have new insight and the Holy Spirit will guide you to the full potential God has for you. A positive mental attitude and a strong desire will allow God to work through you. As a result, you will achieve great things for him.

6

❧Imagination☙

*And the whole earth was of one language, and of one
speech. And it came to pass, as they journeyed from the
east, that they found a plain in the land of Shinar; and
they dwelt there. And they said one to another, Go to,
let us make brick, and burn them thoroughly. And they
had brick for stone, and slime had they for mortar. And
they said, Go to, let us build us a city and a tower, whose
top may reach unto heaven; and let us make us a name,
lest we be scattered abroad upon the face of the whole
earth. And the Lord came down to see the city and the
tower, which the children of men builded. And the Lord
said, Behold, the people is one, and they have all one
language; and this they begin to do: and now nothing
will be restrained from them, which they have imagined
to do. Go to, let us go down, and there confound their
language, that they may not understand one another's
speech. So the Lord scattered them abroad
from thence upon the face of all the earth:
and they left off to build the city.*

Genesis 11:1-8 KJV [Emphasis addded]*

Our mind is where the treasures of life begin. It is where
dreams and ideas start. Anything that we can imagine, we
can do! Through our imagination, God has provided the
path for humans to accomplish more in the last 200 years
than ever before. Not only have we taken over the sky,
but we can fly farther and faster than any bird. We have
even put man onthe moon! Because of modern technology,
we can connect with people from all over the world in a
matter of seconds. We are only limited by our imagination.

*Note: The annotation scripture is merely being used to describe the
power of imagination followed by action. What was going on at the
tower of Babel was not of God. It was a bad thing these people were
doing. The power of our imagination can go, like most things in life, in
two different directions. We are to use our imagination to bring about
good in the lives of mankind. So that we will be uplifting and edifying to
our fellow man; thereby bringing glory to God in all that we do.

All of the greatest accomplishments throughout history were spawned in man's imagination. The Wright Brothers and Henry Ford had a few things in common and one of the biggest was their imagination. Before they could ever build an airplane or an automobile they first had to imagine it. No other creature can do this. We were given dominion over the earth, (cf. Gen. 1:26) we are able to think about our origins and to wonder about our existence, (cf. Psalm 8:4). Only man has this ability. Because we were created in God's Image, we also share some of God's characteristics and one of those is the desire to create. We create using our imagination.

To imagine something is to form a mental picture in your mind about whatever it is you're envisioning. As we mature in the word and forge a closer relationship with God, he will speak to us in that still small voice; the whisper with which he came to Elijah in 1 Kings 19:12. The Holy Spirit will be our constant companion and as we learn to defeat the flesh and follow after the spirit, God will place ideas and thoughts within us. That's the beginning to finding our talents and gifts.

As I stated in the previous chapter, the biggest difference between a victorious individual and one who is defeated is in how they think. However, an even bigger factor is what they do with their thoughts. At some point, we must act on the thoughts that God places within us.

Sometimes we don't always make it the first try. There are always going to be trials and tribulations, and yes, even some failures. By staying focused on God, it will be during these trials, tribulations and failures that we acquire and develop the tools needed to carry out our destiny. Tools such as persistence, patience, determination, time management, money management and the ability to understand what it means to serve others. The person with the defeated mentality will give up at the first signs of trouble and discomfort. The person who is bound and determined to be a success at life will see trouble and failure as an opportunity to learn and to improve themselves. Nothing is wrong with failure as long as we learn from it. A certain amount of failure is necessary as we progress through life. To overcome failure through persistence is to grow as a person; failure is a building block of character.

There is the story of one man who wanted to live life to the fullest. He didn't want his passion and dreams to die with him when his life was over. He wanted to live up to his true potential and allow his gifts to be used in some great way. He was born into poverty; his mother died when he was a child. In the beginning he wasn't sure what his gift was, but rather than stand on the sidelines he chose to take a leap of faith and get into the game of life; to contribute something to mankind while he was here. He decided to take up storekeeping, but the store failed. In fact, the local sheriff had to confiscate his goods and sell them due to his bankruptcy. He decided to take up surveying, but that didn't succeed either. He later joined a group of ragtag soldiers in the Indian Wars as a captain, but his leadership skills were lacking. So, when he reenlisted they demoted him to private. He fell in love and was engaged to be married, but the girl he loved died; leaving him lonely and in a state of shock. This man not only failed twice in business, but also lost eight elections while running for public office. He even suffered a nervous breakdown.

Is it anything short of amazing that Abraham Lincoln became our 16th president? There is a lot to be said for persistence when following your ambitions. If Lincoln had given up, the United States would have missed out on one of its greatest presidents and his contributions to this country would have been lost forever. Mr. Lincoln had the ability to imagine what he wanted. Through imagination and dogged persistence, he was able to become one of the greatest men in American history. He not only had thoughts and imagination, he did something about them. He didn't look at where he came from; he paid no attention to how poor he was. Instead, he looked ahead and plotted a course of action that aligned with his thoughts and imagination and then pressed forward towards his goals.

Ideas are simply the products of our imaginations. From simple ideas, persistent people have made great things happen throughout history.

Imagine right now as you are reading this, what are some things God can accomplish through you? Don't think about where you're at now; just imagine where you would like to be in life. Now ask yourself, what it will take to get there? Do you need to be more active in church? Take some leadership classes? Volunteer more in your town? Run for city council where God will have a voice in your community? Do you need to study more? Do you need to cut spending and save money? Perhaps you need to change your diet and exercise more? Do you need to get out of a toxic relationship?

Right now, your mind is likely coming up with ideas on where to start, so resolve to be one of the successful people and begin to move forward in life. Imagine where you are going. Then, take the thoughts and ideas and put them on paper along with a plan of action that will get the ball rolling. Lastly, allow it to happen.

Through your imagination and dogged persistence, you can discover your talents and achieve anything you want with God in the lead. At this very moment, success or failure is in your hands. Today is the first day of the rest of your life, so make it count!

Self-improvement gurus talk about the universe and how by harnessing its power and its energy it can help you to get whatever you want. They talk about the concept of "me" and how we can get whatever we desire, such as riches and fame. But they fail to mention God created the universe and the laws that govern it. Whatever you imagine and achieve through hard work and a positive mental attitude, the credit goes to God. The rewards are to be shared; because it's not just about us or "me," it's about bringing glory to God and helping others with the blessings he gives us. Without him none of this would be possible. Amen.

THE EMOTIONS AREN'T ALWAYS IMMEDIATELY SUBJECT TO REASON, BUT THEY ARE ALWAYS IMMEDIATELY SUBJECT TO ACTION.

—William James

7

⮜Our Emotions⮞

All Scripture is given by inspiration of God,
and is profitable for doctrine,
for reproof, for correction,
for instruction in righteousness,
that the man of God may be complete,
thoroughly equipped
for every good work.

2 Timothy 3:16-17 NKJV

Emotions are not premeditated, they are a combustion of thoughts and feelings that burst into consciousness suddenly, rather than being planned or thought out. Feelings of joy, anger, sadness, or love along with all emotions will usually be followed by physical changes within the body. Joy and happiness can bring laughter; love will make you experience euphoria. Anger will cause your heart rate to climb leading to mental anguish, along with physical stress and anxiety.

Emotions are a product of the way we think about ourselves, our situations and the world in general. Emotions can drive people to achieve the greatest things in life and they can literally rip people's lives apart. Being well balanced as a Christian starts with our spiritual life, daily renewing our minds as a result of our life in Christ. As we grow in Christ and begin to mature spiritually and mentally our emotions will mature as well. Through the Holy Spirit, we'll begin to experience love, peace and joy.

The different emotional states we experience over the course of our life is greatly impacted by the relationships we form. Sometimes it can be impacted by the lack of relationships. I have seen people who have no social life at all; they stay in the house watching television and reality starts to get confused with fantasy. Being socially active is crucial to our health. Getting involved with other people and having a strong social network is one of the best things we can do for our emotional, spiritual and mental health. Children and adults both can have a difficult time developing good social skills by being alone too much. Kids who are not allowed to be social as they grow up can feel alienated from others. In addition, this isn't limited to children; even adults can develop awkward and shy habits and feel alienated as they grow older as a result of not interacting with others on a regular basis. God created us to fellowship with each other and consequently we need close intimate relationships to function properly. Love is something that we need to give and to receive; the only way to do this is to form relationships with other people.

There are also bad relationships. Sometimes we get involved with people who are toxic and poisonous. These are people who can be controlling, mean and vicious. Sometimes they become people who are very clingy and/or needy. Some people are good *actors*, they have the ability to deceive; they pretend to love you or to be your friend when in reality they are using you. They are around long enough to get their needs met then they are gone. The truly frightening people are those people who react out of severe anger, simply because they have no boundaries and no control over themselves or the words they speak. Anger results in your space being invaded. Whatever the case may be, people who are toxic always want and need more, never being satisfied. They will drain you to the point you have nothing left to give, then they drop you and move on to the next person who can fulfill their needs. It is one thing to try to be there for a friend or partner, but there comes a time when you have to determine whether or not this person sincerely wants to change. We can't change anyone, nor should we try, at least not to the point that our life starts getting out of control. Change has to come from within.

A person has to realize there is a need for change and then they have to want to change. These toxic, poisonous relationships have to be dealt with—one bad apple can spoil the whole barrel. One toxic relationship can ruin your whole life.

We should try to surround ourselves with wise, Godly people. You can tell who they are by the fruit they bear. Their life is disciplined and they have their priorities in order: they put God first. The fruit of their lips will be encouraging, uplifting and positive. People meeting this description will more often than not have a wise counsel.

For a good tree does not bear bad fruit, nor does a bad tree bear good fruit. For every tree is known by its own fruit. For men do not gather figs from thorns, nor do they gather grapes from a bramble bush. A good man out of the good treasure of his heart brings forth good; and an evil man out of the evil treasure of his heart brings forth evil. For out of the abundance of the heart his mouth speaks, (cf. Luke 6:43-45 NKJV).

By having a healthy strong social network and being a part of a body, we can remain spiritually, mentally and emotionally strong, so that in turn we can help someone else who is struggling.

Our emotions and mindset dictate the way we act and come across to others. We want others to see Christ in us and to inquire about the happiness and quality that we experience in our everyday lives. The way we feel inside emotionally shows on our face and in our voice. This will have a direct impact on what doors are opened to you, and what doors remain closed as you pursue your new life and as you begin to learn about your new identity. Having a smile on your face, being happy and positive will draw people to you like a magnet. They will feel better about themselves as a result of being with you. Working well with others and learning to serve happily will make you a leader and open doors of opportunity that you never knew were there. Look at the people you encounter on a daily basis, for example, the guy with the scowl on his face. He has stamped on his forehead: don't come near me, stay away, my walls are up, I don't want to be your friend. This guy is planting seeds of loneliness and heartache. The walls he is putting up are meant to defend him against pain, heartache and rejection, but those same walls will also block out happiness. Unless he lets down those walls and allows someone in, loneliness, pain, rejection and heartache are exactly what he's going to reap. Think about the person who is always upbeat and smiles a lot. She has a positive outlook and everything always seems to work out for her. She is quick with a compliment or a word of encouragement. People enjoy being around her because they feel good about themselves after being in her company: they walk away from the encounter feeling blessed. When you are quick with a smile, a handshake and a kind word, think of it as planting seeds. You are sowing seeds of love, compassion, friendliness and trust. By doing this you will harvest those same qualities from other people. Whether you're new at church and trying to meet people, looking for a new business partner or trying to find that significant other, the way you feel emotionally will manifest itself in your facial expressions, your tone of voice and your body language. All of which speak volumes about your overall character. This in turn will have a direct affect on how you are received and treated by others. If you want to be happy and successful, invest in the happiness and success of others.

When God created us, he gave each one of us our very own personality. Nobody thinks and feels exactly the way you do. Each of us has his or her own way of reacting to situations such as anger, heartache, love and the many other aspects of life. Emotional stability is what will help you to react in a positive way to the circumstances surrounding you. Having a healthy mindset through a healthy spiritual life is the key to being emotionally healthy. The primary emotion that is to be strived for as Christians is love.

When we deal with people on a daily basis, it's an opportunity, to model Christ and come from a place of love and patience. Og Mandino in his book, *The Greatest Salesman in the World* wrote that we should greet each day with love in our heart. The scripture below sums it up pretty nicely:

Whoever does not love does not know God, because God is love. This is how God showed his love among us: he sent his one and only Son into the world that we might live through him. This is love: not that we loved God, but that he loved us and sent his Son as an atoning sacrifice for our sins. Dear friends, since God so loved us, we also ought to love one another. No one has ever seen God; but if we love one another, God lives in us and his love is made complete in us. We know that we live in him and him in us, because he has given us of his Spirit. And we have seen and testify that the Father has sent his Son to be the Savior of the world. If anyone acknowledges that Jesus is the Son of God; God lives in him and he in God. And so we know and rely on the love God has for us. God is love. Whoever lives in love lives in God and God in him, (*cf.* 1 John 4:8-16 NIV).

When we have a healthy, Godly, state of mind; our emotional state will be stable. To be led by the Spirit is to receive the fruit of the Spirit. The qualities that we will experience as a result of a strong spiritual life are detailed in the scripture below.

But the fruit of the Spirit is love, joy, peace, patience, kindness, goodness, faithfulness, gentleness and self-control. Against such things there is no law. Those who belong to Christ Jesus have crucified the sinful nature with its passions and desires. Since we live by the Spirit, let us keep in step with the Spirit. Let us not become conceited, provoking and envying each other, (*cf.* Gal. 5:22-26 NIV).

We can have all of these when we develop the discipline to squash our flesh and allow ourselves to be led by the spirit. This can be achieved by staying strong spiritually which in turn is done by keeping our mind and thoughts turned towards God. Seeking him in everything we do looking for him everywhere we go.

When you look at the opposite of what Paul described what you'll uncover are the unhealthy negative emotions and lifestyle that result from walking after the flesh:

> The acts of the sinful nature are obvious: sexual immorality, impurity and debauchery; idolatry and witchcraft; hatred, discord, jealousy, fits of rage, selfish ambition, dissensions, factions and envy; drunkenness, orgies, and the like. I warn you, as I did before, that those who live like this will not inherit the kingdom of God, (cf. Gal. 5:19-21 NIV).

As stated in the scriptures above, to follow after the flesh causes you to experience emotions such as, anger envy, selfishness, hatred and a host of other negative feelings. These are all based on the ego, and your ego wants you to be in constant struggle with yourself. Your ego will always tell you that you're never good enough, smart enough, slender enough, pretty enough, or strong enough, to accomplish the things you want in life. Your ego wants to always get in the last word and never be wrong. Staying strong spiritually, mentally and emotionally will become easier as you develop the ability to let go of your ego.

When we are bearing those emotions described as the fruit of the spirit, we will be less likely to suffer any long term and habitual mental weakness during trying times, such as depression, sadness, defeat, fear, and hopelessness. We will be more likely to handle the trials and tribulations of life in a healthy and stable way when they come. By having complete control over your emotions and keeping a level head when everybody around you is losing theirs, you can oftentimes defuse a combustible situation and keep it from escalating.

A fool shows his annoyance at once, but a prudent man overlooks an insult, (*cf.* Prov. 12:16 NIV).

Like a city whose walls are broken down is a man who lacks self-control, (*cf.* Prov. 25:28 NIV).

Being optimistic, radiating a positive attitude, is vital to our mental and emotional health. Optimism and a positive attitude are products of faith and hope. No matter what we face or how many setbacks we encounter as we try to fulfill our potential in life, faith, hope and love are the traits that will keep us on a course of true north when nothing else seems to be going right, especially love.

If I speak in the tongues of men and of angels, but have not love, I am only a resounding gong or a clanging cymbal. If I have the gift of prophecy and can fathom all mysteries and all knowledge, and if I have a faith that can move mountains, but have not love, I am nothing. If I give all I possess to the poor and surrender my body to the flames, but have not love, I gain nothing. Love is patient, love is kind. It does not envy, it does not boast, it is not proud. It is not rude, it is not self-seeking, it is not easily angered, it keeps no record of wrongs. Love does not delight in evil but rejoices with the truth. It always protects, always trusts, always hopes and always perseveres. Love never fails. But where there are prophecies, they will cease; where there are tongues, they will be stilled; where there is knowledge, it will pass away. For we know in part and we prophesy in part, but when perfection comes, the imperfect disappears. When I was a child, I talked like a child, I thought like a child, I reasoned like a child. When I became a man, I put childish ways behind me. Now we see but a poor reflection as in a mirror; then we shall see face to face. Now I know in part; then I shall know fully, even as I am fully known. And now these three remain: faith, hope and love. But the greatest of these is love, (*cf.* 1 Cor. 13:8-13 NIV).

It has been suggested in many spiritual writings that we adults should be more like children with our feelings. If you ever sit and watch kids play, you could learn a few things. When we were children we knew how to be real. We hadn't yet been programmed to think masculine or feminine, in the terms of "I'm better than you," or "you're not as strong as me." We were ourselves because we didn't know yet how to put on airs and be who we weren't. No matter how unhealthy it is, men try to hide their emotions and feelings, somewhere along the way we were taught that allowing our emotions to be seen is not the masculine thing to do. Women want men who are strong and stable, men who are whole and well balanced. Men see emotions and crying as signs of weakness, but in reality that is true strength. Being able to talk, communicate and show emotions while still being comfortable with your masculinity is a sign of amazing strength, not weakness. Women today have to be strong in ways that they weren't intended to be, because of the breakdown of families, and because of a lack of mentally and emotionally stable men.

Spiritual, mental, and emotional strength and stability are necessary for both men and women. If you're a woman, and a healthy well-balanced man is what you are asking from God, realize you must also be a healthy, strong, well-balanced woman. Someone once wrote,"A woman's heart should be so lost in God that a man needs to seek him in order to find her," this makes a valid point.

If you're looking for *Mr. Right* and it seems he is not out there, you're possibly focusing on the wrong things. Forget about looking for him and focus on yourself. What I mean by this is that you must seek God first and through him improve yourself. It's very important to work on self-improvement and to build your character so when God puts the right guy in your path, you'll have the spiritual, mental and emotional tools in place to allow the relationship to grow. If you're lugging around a lot of emotional baggage and struggling spiritually, how will you bring anything of value to a relationship when you can't get a handle on yourself? This goes for men and women both. We go from one relationship to the next, not understanding why they never work out. If you don't stop and take a hard, honest close look at yourself, then you'll just keep dragging problems from one relationship to the next. Each time the problems compound until there's no hope left. We have to fix ourselves through God so that he can bless us with the things we desire. A happy, healthy life full of love and prosperity is what he wants for us; but he will not give us these things until we develop the character to manage them.

> Beloved, I pray that you may prosper in all things and be in health, just as your soul prospers, (*cf.* 3 John 1:2 NKJV).

Many Christian women today attempt to recognize the husband as the head of the wife, just as Jesus is the head of the church (*cf.* Eph. 5:22-24). Christian women try to practice submission, but their men have no idea what this means. When a wife submits it means that she respects her husband and allows him to be a husband and a father— she loves and supports him and conducts herself in public with dignity and honor because she is representing not only herself and God, but her husband and children as well. It doesn't mean that the husband rules the house like a tyrant or that he has a corner on all the decisions. It means that his part is to lay down his life for her and he is to give her the love and compassion that Jesus gives to the church, (*cf.* Eph. 5:25-29).

Decisions should be mutually discussed and agreed upon [this is where good communication skills come in]. The husband can set a good example by honoring whatever it is they decide to do, instead of bullying her to get what he wants just because he's bigger, stronger and louder. In exchange, the wife submits herself to him by loving and honoring him; by being a good representative of him and the family. Every word the husband and wife speak and everything they do, whether in public or private reflects on themselves and the entire family.

For the man to be a leader in his home he is to serve his wife and family. Through serving he will be seen as a leader and viewed as a man of strength and character by his wife. But many unhappy men have no idea where they came from, or where they're going; they have lost their identity. They have no direction in life and don't understand that the way to lead is through serving. Many young men today are growing up with poor communication skills and an inability to show any emotion outside of anger and/or frustration. And popular culture through movies and music reinforces this. Sometimes this leads to drug abuse, alcoholism and pornography; which are all used to escape reality. It has been said that, the main thing women want and need is "a man who is stronger than they are." A man who is strong spiritually, mentally and emotionally. Why would they want a man who is weak? A man who is weak, prone to giving into ideas and practices that are not of God, will fail to be an example to his children or his wife. One of the best things a man can do for his children is to love their mother. The same principle applies for women. Women need to constantly set an example for their kids. She must show her daughter how a woman is to be treated. She must show her son how to treat a woman. She does both of these things through example.

When we were kids we didn't stumble around confused over these things. When a child gets hurt he cries, when she needs something she asks for it. When they are happy they laugh out loud, they sing and dance and just have fun. Children get hurt physically or emotionally by another child and it is forgotten in less than thirty minutes. If you see a seven-year old get a spanking from one of his parents, he'll cry, but within a short time he'll give that parent a big hug and go on his way. Everything will be forgiven and forgotten, with no hard feelings or grudges. Children are amazingly in touch with their emotions. They are so full of love and joy that they are quick to forgive and move on. Strengthen yourself emotionally. Stay strong. Doing this is only a matter of making up your mind to do it and then doing it. I know that makes it sound easier than it really is, but in a nutshell that's all there is to it. Some people are stronger than others; some will allow just about anything to roll off of their shoulders and others will collapse into a heap of miserable goo at the tiniest thing. If someone is rude to you and says mean, hurtful things to you, just realize that it's not about you. There is no good excuse for anyone to do that and whatever their problem is they had it before you came along. You just happened to be the recipient at this particular point in time; tomorrow it'll be somebody else.

If you are struggling with your emotions, spend the next 20 minutes filling your mind with something positive. It could be your favorite Bible scriptures, a daily devotional or some motivational reading material. Praise and worship music in your car is also very uplifting and motivating. When you finish, be sure to pray, let God know that you forgive any and everyone who has done you wrong. Forgive yourself for past mistakes and ask him to forgive you of your sins. Before you ask him to forgive you, make sure you have no unforgiveness in your heart. Invite God to search your heart just as David did in Psalm 139:23-24. Only ask him once and then accept it and thank him for it. Thank him for the emotional healing that he has just given to you over the last twenty minutes and welcome it as a gift from the Lord to you. In Jesus name, Amen.

When you face a major problem, stay away from words and phrases that carry weakness and defeat. Don't say "I only have bad luck" or "Nothing good ever happens to me." Whatever you think in your mind and confess with your mouth will eventually come to pass. Use words and phrases that carry strength and power. Use the word of God, for example "I can do all things through Christ who strengthens me," (cf. Phil. 4:13 NIV).

What, then, shall we say in response to this? If God is for us, who can be against us? He who did not spare his own Son, but gave him up for us all—how will he not also, along with him, graciously give us all things? Who will bring any charge against those whom God has chosen? It is God who justifies. Who is he that condemns? Christ Jesus, who died—more than that, who was raised to life—is at the right hand of God and is also interceding for us. Who shall separate us from the love of Christ? Shall trouble or hardship or persecution or famine or nakedness or danger or sword? As it is written: For your sake we face death all day long; we are considered as sheep to be slaughtered. No, in all these things we are more than conquerors through him who loved us. For I am convinced that neither death nor life, neither angels nor demons, neither the present nor the future, nor any powers, neither height nor depth, nor anything else in all creation, will be able to separate us from the love of God that is in Christ Jesus our Lord, (*cf.* Rom. 8:31-39 NIV).

Remember that fear, anger, sadness, jealousy and hopelessness are emotions that come as a result of mental/emotional insecurity and spiritual immaturity. These emotions are perfectly natural in small doses and when kept in check. When these feelings get out of hand they can lead to depression and in severe cases when people get trapped in their minds it can even result in serious psychological problems.

This describes a woman I once knew. She had never been educated in the ways that the word can heal; she believed in God, but never knew him on an intimate level. She lacked that strong social network of Godly people, so she never had anyone to share with her the knowledge she needed to grow spiritually. Some bad things happened that were out of her control. She didn't know how to cope mentally and emotionally. I would often sit and talk with her; we would chat on the phone and sometimes share a meal together. Eventually her mind began to allow sadness to linger longer than it should have, resulting in depression and anxiety. She sought help from the only place she knew: medical doctors. She underwent electric shock treatments, followed by prescription drugs that altered her moods. Because she didn't have the foundation, or the right weapons needed to raise her up and propel her forward, she kept stumbling backwards. Slowly over time, so gradual and subtle were the changes; she most likely never knew it was happening. Then finally she stepped off backwards and plummeted into that deep, dark place that we know as the mind. She was gone, lost forever, never to be heard from again.

What was lost was that part of her that wanted to achieve; the part that drives the rest of us to succeed and to strive to be better every day than we were the day before. I would visit her from time to time and looking back, I'm saddened that the part of her that contained her potential, the part of her that God was trying to work in, was lost. She lived the rest of her life on prescription drugs. Coffee, cigarettes, television and the occasional visits from family were her only things to look forward to. When she passed away, her potential, her gifts and her talents were buried with her. I know God never left her; he was always there by her side wanting to deliver her, but she never learned how to allow him to work in her life. I know she is with him now living a peaceful joyful life, but she could have had it while she was here in this life if she just knew how. Even if she had known, it wouldn't have been easy by any means. We need God and we need one another.

This story describes the extreme to which some people can sink when they are unequipped with the tools needed to cope emotionally with life's difficulties. It's human nature to try to control every aspect of our life. When we have God in our lives and we realize that we don't have to be in control of everything at all times, that's when we can let go and let God take over and allow him to be in control [as I said earlier, you can "let go and let God" as long as you're doing your part].

We should immerse ourselves in the word; by doing this we will over time develop spiritual strength through the understanding of his word and by claiming the promises that we have through him. Spiritual strength and knowledge will lead to mental and emotional strength and stability. When we cast our fears and worries on him and just let go of them, we find that all things work out for the good. Paul tells us, "And we know that in all things God works for the good of those who love him, who have been called according to his purpose," (cf. Rom. 8:28 NIV). How, when and where are not important nor are they any of our business. Walk by faith and simply trust that when you pray and turn your cares over to Christ that they are being dealt with. Continually feed your mind with positive messages, have faith and hope and walk in love.

When we have problems and we ask God for a solution, we need to learn to believe it even when we don't see it or feel it. If we only believe it when we see it and feel it, then we won't believe it when we don't see it or feel it. In 2 Corinthians 5:7 it declares, "we walk by faith, not by sight." Learn to walk in faith. When you believe it even when you don't see it or feel it, then you've started to walk in faith and to trust in the Lord. And this will be the beginning of magnificent things happening in your life!

8
✥Our Ego✥

*Casting down arguments and every high thing that
exalts itself against the knowledge of God, bringing
every thought into captivity to the obedience of Christ,*

2 Corinthians 10:5 NKJV

Some of us struggle with our ego [actually, all of us have this problem]. We don't know how to let the ego just die. Of course, this is much easier said than done. I know this from personal experience and I'm sure that you see this in your own life as well. So many of us base who we are on other people, places and things; if you identify yourself or base who you are on anything other than God, it's just a matter of time until you're going to be let down in a big way.

We try to base who or what we are and how full our life is, on our house, our job, our spouse, how much money we make, our job title, having a slim physique, who we are seen with, our circle of friends, having a fancy or fast car, or sometimes both! Every single one of these *things* are based on ego. During the course of our lives, at least two or more of these will be lost or will change, at the very least. What happens to our ego when we lose a job or take a cut in pay? Or when a divorce comes? Or we lose a friend because of some silly dispute? What happens is our ego takes a direct hit. And if you remember, the ego never wants us to be happy. Our ego tells us that we always have to be right, it tells us that we're not good enough or that people are talking, we have to hurry and create a lie, come up with a story to make us look good, make sure people know it wasn't our fault. The feelings of pain, insecurity, embarrassment and anger start to flood our mind causing a torrent of emotions. This can all be avoided simply by realizing we are a brand new person in Christ.

As Christians, we now have a new identity and a new way of centering ourselves; to center ourselves is to make our thoughts, words and actions parallel the word of God. The way we think, the fruit of our lips and the way we conduct ourselves, in public and private, will easily fit within the pages of the Bible. Your old self is now dead. It is forever gone! "Therefore, if anyone is in Christ, he is a new creation; the old has gone, the new has come," (*cf.* 2 Cor. 5:17 NIV).

When situations spark negative emotions, realize that it's your ego trying to resurrect the old you. In Romans 7:15 Paul talks about his struggle with the flesh, which is what the ego is based on; Paul said, "I do not understand what I do. What I want to do I do not do, but what I hate I do." But you now have Christ at the center of your life and all of these other things take a back seat to him. Squashing our ego, overcoming our flesh and mastering sin is an ongoing struggle, but in Christ we can have the victory. He is at the center and the rest of your life revolves around that fact. This doesn't mean that none of these things will ever happen to you again; it just simply means that when they do, you'll have the mental and emotional fortitude to handle them with grace and poise, while still maintaining your dignity and character. Sure it'll hurt and be hard, but with Christ at the center of your life, you'll know that these things were lost only to make room for something better that is to come.

For a lot of us, our lives are based on the way our parents lived. We don't have to base ourselves on who our parents are or how they lived because we have a new identity in Christ. Realize that your place in society or your current circumstances do not dictate who you are. Never allow your control over your emotions to become weak. Remember,

God is not the author of confusion, so even if you don't know exactly where he's taking you, don't allow the emotions of stress, anxiety, anger and embarrassment to get the best of you. Remember to fight the good fight of faith and to follow God's lead. Paul tells us, "...faith comes by hearing, and hearing by the word of God," (*cf.* Rom. 10:17 NKJV). Whatever emotional trials you go through, rejoice, confident they will make you stronger, (*cf.* James 1:2-4). The best way to determine if you're growing is observing how you handle the next onslaught of negative circumstances. Character is built when you allow yourself to be forged and tempered by the fires of life.

We should also recognize when someone else's ego is lashing out at us and realize that we don't have to allow someone else's opinion of us dictate how we live or to become our reality. When adversity comes, welcome it because adversity is not only how we learn and grow, but it's also how we gauge how much growth we've already achieved. Adversity, if handled correctly, is always followed by victory.

God is not weak nor does he tremble at signs of trouble. He is the ruler of heaven and earth. You are made in his image. He is your Daddy. Therefore, you shouldn't worry during times of trouble either. Keep your emotions in check at all times, hold your thoughts captive and be strong, be courageous and allow the Holy Spirit to be your guide through good times and bad.

MANY SO-CALLED SPIRITUAL PEOPLE,
THEY OVEREAT,
DRINK TOO MUCH,
THEY SMOKE AND DON'T EXERCISE.
BUT THEY DO GO TO CHURCH EVERY
WEEK AND PRAY "PLEASE HELP MY
ARTHRITIS. PLEASE HELP ME BRING UP
MY STRENGTH,
MAKE ME YOUNG AGAIN.

—Jack LaLanne

9
❧Physical Health❧

Do you not know that your body
is a temple of the Holy Spirit,
who is in you, whom you have received from God?
You are not your own; you were bought at a price.
Therefore honor God with your body.

1 Corinthians 6:19-20 NIV

The creation of our bodies is pure and simple a work of wonder, awe and art. Consider our birth and how God designed everything to work just right; how the egg is fertilized and starts out so small inside of a mother's womb and grows from there to become the most capable and intelligent creation in the universe. David marveled at Gods handiwork when he thought about the human body and its intricate design.

> You made all the delicate, inner parts of my body and knit me together in my mother's womb. Thank you for making me so wonderfully complex! Your workmanship is marvelous—how well I know it. You watched me as I was being formed in utter seclusion, as I was woven together in the dark of the womb. You saw me before I was born. Every day of my life was recorded in your book. Every moment was laid out before a single day had passed. How precious are your thoughts about me, O God. They cannot be numbered! I can't even count them; they outnumber the grains of sand! And when I wake up, you are still with me!, (*cf.* Psalm 139:13-18 NLT).

David knew how spectacular and artistically God had crafted us and his finite mind struggled to comprehend it. Our physical well-being is crucial to us being the people God wants us to be. Although physical exercises such as running, weightlifting and other things we do to keep our bodies fit are without a doubt important, I think it's equally important to examine something many of us take for granted: our brain. When we consider the human brain there are simply no words with the power to fully describe its design. Our brain connects to our central nervous system and controls every single body function that we perform. Even when we lift weights the brain comes into play. The heavy overload attacks the central nervous system, which in turn causes the pituitary glands to release more testosterone into the blood stream, which in turn makes allowances for the repair, growth and strength of the muscles—they adapt to the new overload that is being placed upon them.

There has been a lot of debate about the mind, body and spirit. Where does the spirit live? Does it live in our hearts or in our cerebral cortex? What about the mind and the brain? Are they two separate things or are they the same thing? When we speak of the "mind" it connotes consciousness or thoughts and feelings or something of a spiritual nature; when we speak of the "brain," we think of something that is more physical that is used to control the body. I believe that they are one and the same, or two aspects of the same thing. When you look at the mind/brain scenario, it's as if there are many parts that make up the whole.

Earlier I talked about our mind and how we use it to control our emotions and how the renewing of it helps with our spiritual lives. I'm now going to discuss the physical aspects of the mind/brain.

When we think of our bodies and taking care of them we normally think about diet and exercise. These are important, but let us not forget that our brains are also a part of our body. It's a part that most people never consider. We use our brain to think, but we never think of our brain! It needs to be worked just like the rest of our body. Reading, solving puzzles and interacting with others in a social setting is very important to our spiritual, mental and emotional health. Such activities stimulate our brains. In the cortex of the brain there are areas with deep wrinkles, which give our brain more surface area. Some theorize that it's because of the wrinkles and the amount of surface area we have that we get our intelligence. Whatever the case, we need to keep our brains sharp and healthy as we age. Reading, socializing, learning and problem solving are all things that keep our brain sharp and healthy. The brain is without question, the most amazing and complicated of all God's designs. We possess in our skull the most complicated computer ever designed. Throughout our lifetime, we continually are adding new programs to it.

The brain is made up of five parts, the biggest being the cerebrum. The cerebrum—also known as the cortex—is about 85 percent of the brain's total weight. It is broken down into smaller sections called lobes, which control all of our thoughts, reasoning, problem-solving and visual abilities. The cerebrum controls both long and short-term memory. It controls the voluntary muscles used in activities such as running, working and weight lifting. Half of the cerebrum is on one side of your head and half is on the other side. Medical science has determined that the left side of your cerebrum controls the right side of your body. The right side of your cerebrum controls the left side of your body. Scientists believe that one side is for problem solving and speech while the other side determines shapes and colors. Its distinctive wrinkles give it more surface area, which is thought to make it more efficient.

The cerebellum is located at the back of the brain. It's smaller than the cerebrum and is responsible for our sense of balance: it keeps us walking upright. Damage to this part of the brain results in staggering, sluggish movements and weakened muscles. The brain stem connects the rest of the brain to the spinal cord. It controls blood flow, digestion and breathing; all of which involve involuntary muscles.

The brain stem keeps these functions in operation without us ever having to think about them.

The hypothalamus controls body temperature, which is somewhere around 98.5 degrees Fahrenheit. It tells our bodies to tremble or to sweat, whichever is necessary to regulate our body temperature. The hypothalamus is located in the middle of the base of the brain, just above the pituitary gland. The Pituitary gland is about the size of a small pea and it controls the release of hormones into the body. It also regulates our metabolism so our bodies have the energy they need to function properly.

Our brain controls how we think, feel, move, see, hear, taste and smell. The brain uses approximately 20 percent of the oxygen that we breathe in and 20 percent of our blood flow. Believe it or not, our brain boasts thousands of miles of interconnected nerve cells—approximately 100 billion—that control every thought, movement and emotion that relates to our life. When the brain and spinal cord are combined, there are thousands of varieties of neurons with support cells numbering in the trillions. Scientists have not yet begun to fully understand the human brain and probably never will. The complex design of the human brain is simply beyond human comprehension. Only God knows all of the intricate details of the brain, because he is its designer and creator.

These brief descriptions of the brain and its components give us an idea of its design and importance. Whether we feel anger or pain, hot or cold, these are all regulated by our brains. Therefore, whatever we feed our minds and bodies is interconnected and has a huge impact on how we feel and view the world. Just like our muscles, we also need to exercise our brains. One way is to learn a new language, or learning anything new for that matter. Try to read and learn something new each day. It's been said that learning a new language or a new skill can help to slow down dementia. Brain exercises are a great way to stay alert nd strong. There are programs designed for your brain hat can help improve your memory, focus and the ability o think quicker. These different types of brain-training ooks and software can be found all over the Internet.

Diet has a huge impact on our brains as well. Diets high n omega-3 fatty acids found in fish are very nourishing o our brains. A Mediterranean diet focuses on what you *:an* eat verses what you *can't* eat. The Mediterranean style f eating is about foods with healthy fats, Olive oil, more egetables and less meat; which fuels your brain as well as our body. Conversely, eating a diet high in saturated fats —animal products and some oils derived from plants, like alm oil, cocoa butter and coconut oil—will make you feel bsolutely miserable physically and will eventually make us eel bad mentally about ourselves and our circumstances. our brain controls every one of your body functions, so ake the extra time to do the research on how to eat and exercise for a healthy brain.

Stress:

Trust in the LORD with all your heart; do not depend on your own understanding. Seek his will in all you do, and he will show you which path to take, (*cf.* Prov. 3:5-6 NLT).

The LORD is my light and my salvation—so why should I be afraid? The LORD is my fortress, protecting me from danger, so why should I tremble? When evil people come to devour me, when my enemies and foes attack me, they will stumble and fall. Though a mighty army surrounds me, my heart will not be afraid. Even if I am attacked, I will remain confident, (*cf.* Psalm 27:1-3 NLT).

Stress is another area we should try to eliminate from our lives. It is actually more of a mental/emotional problem, but it manifests itself through physical symptoms, which is why I decided to include it here. By working toward making ourselves whole we can help reduce the amount of stress we carry by exercising and taking care of our bodies. When God created us we were not meant to carry the burden of stress. As we age and become more involved and more successful we tend to take on stress and carry it around like some sort of a bad habit. Stress negatively affects us on every level: mentally, emotionally, physically and—if not dealt with—spiritually. I'm talking about the physical aspects of stress here. Stress and anxiety, when carried around for years, can result in anger and depression, which in turn leads to high blood pressure, heart attacks, loss of appetite, loss of sleep, headaches and poor health in general, not to mention a poor outlook on life, which in turn will have a negative affect on how you interact socially. It's been said that if we have the ability to eliminate bad habits then we can also eliminate stress. Anxiety and stress are what make us worry. These are each fear-based problems. They are very subtle and destructive diseases. Norman Vincent Peale wrote, "The word worry is derived from an old Anglo-Saxon term meaning to choke. If someone were to put their hands around your throat and squeeze, cutting off the flow of vital power, it would be a dramatic demonstration of what you do to yourself by long held and habitual worry."

People who experience a lot of stress could dramatically shorten their lives. Find ways to relax such as attending church and prayer. Practice moderation in both working and eating. Those who over eat and/or over work are stressing the mind and body to an early grave. Do something that is fun and enjoyable at least once a day. Eat healthier foods in smaller amounts. Develop the discipline to exercise daily and to read books about your favorite subjects. Get plenty of sleep. There's an old saying that states, "go get some sleep and everything will look better in the morning." This is the truth and it really helps. When you're tired and stressed out and filled with anxiety, all you need sometimes is a good night's rest. When you wake up everything is clear. You can make much better decisions. Plenty of sleep is a must if we are to maintain the physical component of being well-balanced people. It plays a vital role when dealing with stress.

Remember that worry, anxiety and fear are all bad mental habits that will sooner or late wreak havoc on you physically. If Jesus himself walked with you daily, then you would have nothing to fear. So draw closer to him and he will draw closer to you, (*cf.* James 4:8). He will actually walk with you everywhere you go. Affirm to yourself aloud, "God is with me." Do this daily. Accept it as a fact and your reasons for worry will begin to fade away. If God is with you then who or what can stand against you?

All of the systems in the body are interconnected. If people ignore their physical health then their spiritual health, mental health, social health and emotional health will also be negatively affected. Just as depression or any other illness can affect a person's physical well-being, being in poor physical shape can similarly affect all the systems of the body. Eating properly and maintaining an ideal weight will make any stress more tolerable for the body, mind and emotions. Physical fitness will make everything in life easier. It will improve our quality of life, job performance and everything we undertake in life. Our main goal is to serve God. One of the ways we do this is by serving others. Maintaining optimal physical health will give us that mental edge, that energy and drive to do more in the way of being servants. It has been said that our bodies are a space that we occupy while going through this life. Our service to God and service to mankind is the rent we pay for the space we occupy while here on earth.

Exercise:

Don't be impressed with your own wisdom. Instead, fear the Lord and turn away from evil. Then you will have healing for your body and strength for your bones, (*cf.* Prov. 3:7-8 NLT).

Taking care of your body is a wise thing to do. Talk to those who have spent their lives neglecting their physical health and I'm sure they would do things differently if given the chance to start over. Diet and exercise are essential ingredients needed to make life a lot more enjoyable as we age.

Exercising will give you a lean healthy body when coupled with a good all natural-diet. However, a slim, trim physique is just a side benefit and shouldn't be the sole reason we work out. Focusing only on how our body appears would be egotistical. We need to consider how a healthy body makes us feel. The better we feel the more production God can get out of us. The healthier we are the better we will feel. The better we feel the more likely we are to start moving towards our goals. Remembering that we are the glory of God and our bodies are a gift, given to us by God as we travel through this life.

As we have already discovered, we need to be strong in several areas in order to be whole and to allow God to achieve the maximum amount of work through us. In the same way, as a hammer or saw is to the carpenter, we need to be the tools of God. He wants to build the church and make it strong. We can be the tools that he uses to build his church by being examples to others, who see us and desire the peace, joy and happiness that we have [Fruit of the Spirit]. We can be ready to give an answer to anyone who asks about the joy and hope inside of us, (*cf.* 1 Pet. 3:15). Being physically fit will strengthen us mentally and emotionally, which in turn makes it easier to stay strong spiritually. Satan seeks to get a foothold in our lives by attacking us physically, mentally or emotionally which he then uses to weaken us spiritually.

If Satan can't get you spiritually he'll circle around and try to sneak into your life and attack your spirit by going through the back door. Drug abuse, alcoholism, pornography, eating disorders, excessive spending, anger, abuse and depression are all things that can manifest themselves, not only spiritually, mentally and emotionally, but also physically. These are all things that Satan uses to attack us. He doesn't care so much about the addictions themselves; those are just a means to an end. The addictions create a space or a wedge between us and God, which is what Satan really wants. If he can get you addicted to pills or get you addicted to food [comfort food—eating to calm down or to forget], then that can drag down other areas of our life, which causes us to live apart from God's will. These addictions, whether food or drugs or sexual, over time will start to decay our lives and our relationships.

Food addictions will lead to obesity. In just the same way as drugs or alcohol, obesity will eventually break down how we feel about ourselves physically, mentally and emotionally. Going in the opposite direction with body weight is equally as bad. Anorexia results from how people mentally view themselves. Anorexics have a false story in their mind of who they are and how others view them. They believe they are overweight and will go to extreme lengths to stay slim, often becoming emaciated and sometimes dying. Anorexia is an eating disorder that wreaks havoc on the body and all aspects of the personal life of the person suffering, not to mention the pain and fear it inflicts upon those who love them. These unbalances and addictions will lead, over time, to a spiritual breakdown, causing sufferers to wonder why God doesn't hear my prayers? Why does he not answer my prayers? Why doesn't he help me? God doesn't care about me. He doesn't love me anymore. What have I done to deserve this? Why is he punishing me? Why has my family turned their back on me? Why does everyone avoid me? As you can see, through addictions Satan can attack us physically first, then through that he has access to our minds and every single aspect of our lives. No matter how well you take care of yourself mentally and emotionally, Satan will still gain access to you through your physical body if you neglect it.

This brings to mind a story about a man who owned one thousand acres. He sold nine hundred and ninety-nine of them. He kept one acre of land, which was located right in the center of the original thousand acres. The new owner thought to himself, "I have all this land and that guy kept one acre right in the middle. Now I have control over his land and he can't get to it because I will not allow it." The man with the one acre started making a path across the other man's land to gain access to his one acre. The new owner took the man with the one acre to court expecting the law to stop him from building a road across his newly acquired property. However, according to law the new owner had to allow access across his newly bought property so that the man could get to his one acre. No matter what he did or how hard he fought, the courts maintained he had to allow the man to build a driveway across his land in order to get to that one acre. He had to allow an easement, or a right of way.

That's an illustration of how Satan operates. If we take care of ourselves spiritually, mentally and emotionally, but neglect ourselves physically, then we are allowing the evil one access to us through poor health. If Satan can wreck our bodies and health then he, through that, can begin to pull us down in other areas thereby robbing us of our joy, happiness and well-being, not to mention of our destiny. When we give our lives to God we need to give all of it to him, not just a portion of it. Satan wants to keep that one acre of our life so he can maintain access to us. We need to sell out to God, not just part of ourselves, but all of ourselves, spiritually, mentally, emotionally and physically. This needs to be done daily so that God alone will have full access to us.

We were not meant to be sedentary in our physical lives; we were made to worship and we were created to work. When God created Adam the intention was not for Adam simply to sit around and eat, God told him to tend the garden.

The Lord God placed the man in the Garden of Eden to
tend and watch over it, (*cf.* Gen. 2:15 NIV).

This is cut and dried. Man was created, among other
things, for work. God gave to Adam everything he needed,
not just to have life, but also to have life abundantly. But,
this abundant life required work. A healthy diet and hard
work are two key ingredients that will keep us in shape and
physically healthy. These are required in order to achieve
a long and happy life. In the world we live in today, life
has become so easy that we need to assist our bodies with
exercise. There are those who still have hard jobs that
require a lot of hard physical work, but for the rest of us
we need to work our bodies on a regular basis. I believe at
any age above 12, weight lifting is the best as long as you
find someone qualified to show you the proper techniques.

A well-designed program will keep you from suffering
injuries and/or getting burned out from over-doing it.
[Before the age of 12 the best thing for children to be
physically healthy is simply to be outside in the sunshine
and the dirt and the grass playing and interacting with
other children.] From my own experience, weight lifting
will lift your spirit and give you that extra spring in your
step that makes you feel good all over. And just like when
you first gave your life to God, you may or may not have
felt that different at first, but over time it becomes more
and more apparent that changes are taking place. At first
only you and God may notice the subtle changes, because
most of the changes are in the way you think and feel. After
some time immersed in the word and in prayer you begin
to change outwardly as your actions and the words you
speak change. Soon everyone around you begins to notice
the difference.

The same thing happens when you start exercising on
a regular schedule. In the beginning you will be the only
one who notices any changes; simply because in the first

few weeks, most of the changes are not outward, but on the inside, in the way you think and feel. Then your body starts to change and you are feeling so much better, and you smile more and begin to walk with more confidence. You will begin to enjoy increased mental clarity; you'll sleep sounder at night and crave more water and healthier foods.

During the transformation of your physical body, try not to pay attention to the scales, because muscle weighs more than fat and takes up less space. So, even though your weight may not change too much—depending on how overweight or underweight you were to begin with—your body will start to shift its weight to different areas and your clothes will start to get much looser. Trying to keep that certain special weight is not the way to determine your physical well-being; it's much better to go by how you feel and how your clothes fit. Learn to listen to your body and you will know when to pick up the pace and when to slow down a bit.

There was the story of the lady who never exercised and was convinced that all she needed to do was maintain that certain "magical weight" that she had in high school. As she aged she was able to do this. That special number was always there when she stepped on the scales. Sometimes it would go up, but all she had to do was skip a meal or two and it would go right back down, so she was happy. As she began to get in her fifties she didn't feel as good; headaches, lack of sleep, and a loss of energy began to plague her. When she would raise her arm to wave, the flap under her arm would also wave. Her stomach began to get loose as well as her hips and thighs. But every time she stepped on the scales, she would see that "magical weight" and think everything was peachy. What was happening was that as she aged she was losing muscle. Gradually over time her muscle weight was being replaced by more body fat, so her weight didn't go up much, but her body began to shift and her clothes wouldn't fit right and she began to feel bad and had very little energy. What's worse was she started to feel bad about herself. I think this may be one reason why Jesus told us to love our neighbor as ourself; because how can we love and embrace others if we can't love and embrace ourselves?

This isn't about ego, pride or vanity; it's about taking care of our temple. It's about caring for the body that God gave us to walk around in. The healthier you are the better you'll look and feel, and the better you look and feel the more likely you are to step out of your comfort zone and be the man or woman God has destined you to be. There is no way to share with other people the ways God can heal and bless us with good health and prosperity if we are not doing the necessary work to allow him to manifest these things in our own lives. No matter what you may think, I can assure you that the healthier you are and the better you feel, the more you can and will accomplish for God. The better you feel about yourself the more capable you'll be to realize your full potential, and to use the gifts and talents with which God blessed you. Staying fit will help us to stand up strong with confidence and boldness, allowing us to be confident in our abilities and to live up to our full potential, rather than going to the grave and having our dreams buried with us, never realizing what differences God could have made in the world through us. Remember the analogy of the thousand acres? Don't let your physical health be that one acre that allows Satan access to your spirit, mind and emotions.

Research will usually link exercise to good physical health, but exercise is also good for our mental and emotional health as well. Physical exercise causes the body to release endorphins, which make us feel better and happier. Using our muscles sparks a chemical reaction in the body causing our bones to thicken, which is very important as we age and the threat of osteoporosis looms larger.

Tendons and ligaments also thicken, helping to reduce the amount of tears and damage they receive as a result of everyday activities such as, working in the yard, walking and hiking. Exercise will help relieve stress and anxiety. When combined with a healthy diet exercise will help regulate our body weight, which in turn helps to ward off high blood pressure and heart disease. The more body fat we carry the harder it is on our knees, back and joints. Too much body fat also causes our organs to work overtime. A healthy diet is required for normal brain function and general health. Our diet provides us the energy and nutrients we need for exercise and working.

In Leviticus God instructed the Israelites on what they should and should not eat. This diet he gave them is not a salvation issue; it was intended to teach them obedience as well as to keep them healthy. If we were to follow these dietary guidelines we could possibly extend our lives, and increase the quality of our life as well.

Being at a healthy weight and staying in shape is not just about being physically strong and healthy; it's also about feeling good and having the confidence to do the work of the Lord. It plays a role in how we will multiply our talents for the Master and reach our full potential in Christ.

Everything is Spiritual:

We know that being whole and well balanced is what God wants for each one of us. This way God can use us in the way he desires. He wants us to use our talents and live up to our full potential in life. We discussed earlier that taking care of our half of the whole means to develop ourselves in every area of our life. These six areas are listed once again here, and in order of importance—Spiritual, Mental, Emotional, Physical, Social, and Financial.

I listed social and financial as the last two simply because if we take care of the first four aspects of our life, he last two should fall into place naturally. If we allow any two or more of these areas to get out of hand, it can drag he others down over time.

I put spiritual at the top, but here's the deal—they are all spiritual! You can't have a spiritual life that is separate from all other areas of your life. To say that one part of our life is spiritual is to imply that another part is not. We have to make our spirituality a part of every area of our life. If we are working to develop ourselves mentally, emotionally, physically, socially and financially, then we must make God a part of all of these. We are to make God the main focus in every single aspect of our life!

Before you read a book, ask yourself, would God want me to read this? Before you eat your lunch, think to yourself, would he want me to eat this? Before you spend money on something, remember that it's God who blessed you with that money—it belongs to him. So, would God be okay with what I'm about to spend his money on? Before we open our mouth we should think about the words we are speaking; are they uplifting and edifying to the person on the receiving end and those within earshot? Before we make decisions, we should ask ourselves if it's what God wants for us. By asking ourselves these questions, and talking to God about them, we are making every part of our life Spiritual. This will allow us to make better and wiser decisions in every area of our daily life.

At the beginning of this chapter I brought up the topic of where our spirit lives. I have read different ideas on this and asked some friends and family members their opinions on the topic. Most frequently, people will say that our spirit resides in our heart or that it lives in our mind. I listened to one pastor who taught that our spirit lived in the frontal lobes of our brain just behind our eyes. One day I spoke with a friend of mine and she gave a very thought-provoking answer to my simple question: In what part of our body does our spirit reside? She replied, "Our spirit is not dwelling in any single area of our body. It is a part of, and dwells in, every fiber and cell of our being." I thought about this and I would have to agree; it is a part of our entire being. It is written that the life is in the blood, (*cf.* Lev. 17:11).

Stop the flow of blood to anything and it will begin to die. Our spirit and body are linked together; they are woven together and only separated by physical death. So it would seem that our spirit is in our blood coursing through our veins, it is in the bones of our skeletal system, it is a part of our heart, mind/brain, organs and every aspect of our physical body.

Our body and spirit are so interconnected that if we allow our physical health to get to far out of control, we will suffer in other areas of our life. It seems the better we take care of our body, the better we feel spiritually, mentally and emotionally. This doesn't matter if you're at the gym working out, or if you are working in the garden, or mowing the yard. Staying physically active is crucial to our overall well-being. As Christians, it's my conviction that we should take a closer look at this subject, simply because God has a much more difficult time trying to work through someone who consistently feels bad about themselves. It is much easier to be helpful and good to others when we are good to ourselves.

If you have a hard time getting motivated to eat right and to work/exercise, then think about the link between our body and our spirit. If you can find no other reasons to eat right and exercise, then at least try to take care of yourself because in you, is where the Spirit of God resides.

Laughter:
Critical to our spiritual, mental, emotional and physical health is being happy. Find a reason to laugh, look for

easons to smile and enjoy yourself everyday. Being socially active helps us to accomplish this; when we fellowship we are literally pouring from vessel to vessel.

Fellowship and being socially active creates friendships and bonding with others that in turn has a dramatic effect on our overall health and the quality of our life. Laughter eases stress and anxiety. It draws people to you, helps you to relax and feel more at ease. Laughter has even been said to lower blood pressure. Laughter helps you to get out of your mind—it helps you to be increasingly present and available. It is good to laugh as much as possible, when you are in the car, or doing house chores, anytime at all. And it's even better when you're laughing along with others. It is easy to see that laughter is one of the best gifts that God blessed us with. Laughter is a major benefit to every area of your life. Of laughter, it has been said—one minute of anger weakens the immune system for four to five hours and one minute of laughter can boost the immune system for up to 24 hours.

A happy heart makes the face cheerful, but heartache crushes the spirit," (*cf.* Prov. 15:13 NIV).

WATCH YOUR THOUGHTS, FOR THEY
BECOME WORDS.
WATCH YOUR WORDS, FOR THEY
BECOME ACTIONS...

—Origin Unknown

10
❧Words❧

The good man brings good things
out of the good stored up in his heart,
and the evil man brings evil things
out of the evil stored up in his heart.
For out of the overflow of his heart his mouth speaks.

Luke 6:45 NIV

The word *universe* could be defined as everything in the heavens and the earth. It is time, space and matter; and all of the universal laws that God put into place during the creation. The speed of light, speed of sound, gravity and everything that we as humans can measure, study and experience are all part of the universe.

I researched the word *universe* and one source said, "The universe comprises everything we perceive to physically exist, the entirety of space and time, all forms of matter and energy, and the physical laws and constants that govern them." That, to me, was a fitting definition. Another definition that I heard states the universe is everything—everything that ever was, is, or will be. I thought to myself, hmmm, this one is apt as well! It continued by noting that the literal translation of "universe" means "one verse" or "one word."

If you look for the origin of the word *universe*, you'll uncover all kinds of answers. One answer is that "*uni*" means whole or one. The other part of the word "*verse*" means to turn, which translated would mean, *whole turned into one*. This didn't make much sense to me; however, there is another translation to consider, the word "uni" means single, the word "verse" is a spoken sentence. When you look at it in these terms, to say we live in the universe is to say we live in a single spoken sentence—and God said, "Let there be." Everything we know that's good was spoken into existence. With words, God brought forth everything good, which was, is, and is to be.

Genesis chapter 1 tells us how God spoke everything into existence. In verses 26-29 he creates mankind and then he takes a look at all he has created. Then God declares everything he had made was very good!

> Then God said, "Let Us make man in Our image, according to Our likeness; let them have dominion over the fish of the sea, over the birds of the air, and over the cattle, over all the earth and over every creeping thing that creeps on the earth." So, God created man in his *own* image; in the image of God he created him; male and female he created them. Then God blessed them, and God said to them, "Be fruitful and multiply; fill the earth and subdue it; have dominion over the fish of the sea, over the birds of the air, and over every living thing that moves on the earth." And God said, "See, I have given you every herb *that* yields seed which is on the face of all the earth, and every tree whose fruit yields seed; to you it shall be for food. Also, to every beast of the earth, to every bird of the air, and to everything that creeps on the earth, in which *there* is life, I have given every green herb for food"; and it was so. Then God saw everything that he had made, and indeed *it* was very good. So the evening and the morning were the sixth day, (*cf.* Gen. 1:26-29 NKJV). **[Emphasis added]**

In the Gospel of John we also get a look at the importance of the word. "In the beginning was the Word, and the Word was with God, and the Word was God. He was in the beginning with God. All things were made through Him, and without Him nothing was made that was made," (*cf.* John 1:1-3 NKJV).

No matter what you do in this life, no matter who you are, what your background is, or where you come from, the good things as well as the bad are directly related to the way you talk. There is life and death in the words we speak.

We have discussed in previous chapters about how God wants you to realize the talents that he gave you, so that when this life comes to an end you will have multiplied those talents many times, thus reaching your potential in Christ and contributing to mankind in some way during your stay here in this world.

Christians and the church talk about giving, and giving is something Jesus wants us to do, but giving is not just about money. Simply giving money can at times be the easy way out. Giving is not just about money and clothing, or donating food to the local homeless shelter. Yes, these are all forms of giving, but giving is also sharing your gifts and talents with mankind. It can be the music that you always wanted to play, the poetry that you want to write, a piece of art that you create, or maybe an invention that makes life a little more convenient. Whatever your contribution to the rest of us may be, it's a gift. This is a form of giving. This dream, this desire, this longing in your heart, this gift that you have to share with the rest of us, begins with a thought. You imagine it first then you speak it into existence. You verbalize these desires that the Holy Spirit has placed in your heart and in your thoughts. Before God created the universe, he first thought it. He did the same thing with man. He had the thought first when He said let's make man in our image; the statement was a verbal expression of what he was thinking. Then he spoke it, then he saw it; and he saw that it was very good. We should do likewise. When we are following our path in life we should take our goals, write them on paper, confess them with our mouth and then do the necessary work to bring them into existence. By doing this we are using our words in two different ways: we are using the written word by putting them on paper and then we are using the spoken word by verbalizing our goals. This is faith in action! We now see the words, we say the words and we hear the words; all that's left to do is to put the action to the words we have written and spoken.

In the days of Jesus, they understood very well that action was a part of hearing. According to Lois Tverberg and Bruce Okkema, who co-authored *Listening to the Language of the Bible*, "When you see the word listen or hear in the Bible, it is usually a translation of the word *Shema* [pronounced sh'ma]. Shema means to obey; when you run across a scripture in the Bible that says to listen or hear, put the word obey in its place and it takes on a whole new meaning." *Shema* doesn't mean that we just hear or listen; it means that we do, that we obey by doing. When we have eyes to see and ears to hear this means that we put the action to what we have seen and heard. If we say that we see and hear, yet we never do anything, then we have not truly seen or heard, otherwise we would be applying the action to what we have seen and heard by doing something.

When we have desires in our heart from God to achieve certain things in our life, we sometimes feel excited and empowered. We feel as though we can accomplish anything to which we set our minds. We decide to start a business, or begin a new and rewarding career, start eating right and exercising, or maybe write a book. We have this inner voice saying, "Yes! I can do it!" We start planning everything out and thinking about how great it's all going to be! Then after a while the excitement wears off. We start to come back down from this high. We may start to tell ourself that we're coming back down to reality. Suddenly there are different words; there is this inner voice telling us to give up. We might think to ourselves: "I can't, it's too hard; I'm not attractive enough; I'm not smart enough; I don't have enough money; I'm too old. I'm too young; This only works out for other people..." We can think all kinds of defeated excuses. When this happens the words we decide to listen to will become our reality. Developing the spiritual, mental and emotional maturity to stay focused when doubt creeps in is what will pull us through the hard times. Whatever we want to accomplish in life, we can bet there will be resistance. When this happens, speak words of authority over your circumstances.

Wherever you happen to be at this stage of your life is a direct result of every word that you have ever spoken. Our words are a direct result of what's in our heart. That which is in our heart is a direct result of our words: we are what we say. Who you are is in part a reflection of how you believe and act. How you believe and act is a reflection of the words you speak. The words you speak are a reflection of the way you think. The fruit of your lips has a huge impact on how you feel about life, the quality of your life, how others view you and how you are treated. You can change the direction your life is going at this very moment by simply changing your vocabulary. Starting today, make it a point to learn new words, words that speak of strength and life.

If a person is speaking words of anger, hatred, violence and revenge, then that person in his or her mind is already mean, violent and vengeful. When people talk this way, they also tend to act out on their words; they tend to be aggressive and violent in their behavior. The only way they can change is to change their vocabulary and the way they think, but they have to want to change themselves for this to happen. We can't change them because change has to come from within.

If we always talk about being lonely, sad and depressed, we give life to those emotions and we will continue to feel that way. If you are talking this way to your family, friends, coworkers and others, they will begin to view you and to think of you, as sad, lonely and depressed. You are verbally dictating how other people see you. When we speak, our words are like seeds that we sow. Whatever we plant, that is what we are going to reap. The things you fear the most will come upon you when you start speaking them into existence.

I have been around people who always discuss how sick they are and how many medications they're taking.

They will sometimes spend hours talking about and detailing their ailments. When you next get around a group of people like this, note how they seem to feed off one another. Each one will have it a little bit worse than the previous. "I'm so sick, I spend a fortune on medication, my joints are killing me, my back hurts, I have migraines, I've had five surgeries and I need five more." I've even heard some people confessing that their days are numbered and they will not live much longer. I understand we all get sick. We all experience problems here and there as we age, but wallowing in our maladies and sickness by talking this way is giving life to our problems and only making them worse. We should never ignore dangerous health issues, or neglect to take the necessary steps when health problems arise, but sometimes we equate complaining about our problems as doing something about them. Complaining keeps giving power to the problem and it can be a drain on ourselves and upon those who love and care about us.

> Les Brown told a story about a dog that reflects how some of us act at times: "There was a man who stopped at this house to visit the people living there; on the front porch was this old dog that kept moaning and groaning. The man asked the dog's owner, what's wrong with that dog? The owner said, "He is lying on a nail; to which the visitor replied, well, why doesn't he move? The owner said "I guess it doesn't hurt badly enough."

This is exactly how some of us treat life. We can become so comfortable being uncomfortable that we never move. We just complain and we actually see complaining as the same thing as doing something about it.

If and when we find ourselves in the midst of a crisis like divorce, bankruptcy, or even something as serious as cancer, why not try something different for a change? We can acknowledge the problem or the symptoms of our dilemma and take the necessary steps to solve the problem, but at the same time speak words of power and authority over our circumstances.

Have you ever been around people who are hopeful, positive, confident and strong in their manner and speech? No matter how desperate their situations may be, they speak words of love and peace; they are quick with a smile, a word of encouragement and they inspire those around them. This is the stuff of which great leaders are made. Their words are positive and uplifting. They face the same problems in life that the rest of us face, but because of the words they speak, they have developed a level of maturity and discipline that in turn has given them the character to confront their problems with authority and victory.

When we speak strong, victorious, uplifting words we are speaking into existence those things in our life. We are more likely to be treated well by others and feel better about ourselves. Have you ever been around someone who uses profanity constantly? People who use foul language and speak profanity in every sentence are speaking into existence their own filth and dirtiness. The doors of opportunity will hardly ever be open to them. To stop using profanity is to immediately increase your intelligence; simply because when you stop using bad words you have to learn new ones to replace the bad ones just so you can express yourself. Simply changing the way you talk is a quick way to change who you are. As Christ followers, we are commanded to put off the old man and put on the new. We need to leave our old self in the past and renew our minds and become new creatures through Christ. Learning new words and changing the way we communicate with others is a great place to start!

> What goes into a man's mouth does not make him 'unclean,' but what comes out of his mouth, that is what makes him 'unclean,' (*cf.* Matt. 15:11 NIV).

What's in a name?

The importance of the words we use can be seen in the names of some of the greatest men in the Bible. When God called on man to bring about some of the most profound changes, changes that would alter the entire world forever, He had to change the way they spoke, which in turn began to change the way they thought. By doing this God changed their reality, enabling these people to have a change of mind. You could say God renewed their minds making them believe, so God could do his work through them. Changing their names helped them to share the vision that God had for their life and for the world to come.

There was Abram, who is known as the father of Christianity, Judaism and Islam. All three faiths see him as the father of their ancestry. God promised Abram that he would be the father of many nations; however, at this time Abram was 99 years old!

> When Abram was ninety-nine years old, the Lord appeared to him and said, "I am God Almighty; walk before me and be blameless. I will confirm my covenant between me and you and will greatly increase your numbers."Abram fell facedown and God said to him, "As for me, this is my covenant with you: You will be the father of many nations...., (cf. Gen. 17:1-4 NIV).

This promise was made to Abram and his wife Sarai, who were both well past the age of having children. So, the first thing he did, after making this promise to Abram, was to change his name; which is what God does in verse five: God also said to Abraham, "As for Sarai your wife, you are no longer to call her Sarai; her name will be Sarah. I will bless her and will surely give you a son by her. I will bless her so that she will be the mother of nations; kings of peoples will come from her," (cf. Gen. 17:15-16 NIV).

By changing their names, God was changing the way Abraham and Sarah spoke to one another, as well as the way others spoke to them. Abraham and Sarah each harbored doubts about having children because of their age, but when they spoke to one another they were speaking their destiny into existence. Every time Sarah said Abraham's name she was saying father; and every time Abraham said Sarah's name, he was saying mother. Anyone who spoke to them was addressing them as father and mother. They were all speaking what was not as though it was. This is using the power of words and it's a perfect example of faith. When Abraham was about 100 years old, they had a son. Sarah was about 90 years old. Their son was named Isaac.

Abraham had a grandson through Isaac whose name was Jacob. God wanted to make a mighty nation from Jacob; before Abram became Abraham God promised to make a mighty nation from him.

The Lord had said to Abram, "Leave your country, your people and your father's household and go to the land I will show you. I will make you into a great nation and I will bless you; I will make your name great, and you will be a blessing. I will bless those who bless you, and whoever curses you I will curse; and all peoples on earth will be blessed through you, (*cf.* Gen. 12:1-3 NIV).

God made Abraham a promise and this promise was being carried out through Jacob. Once again, we will see that God will change the way the Israelites speak by changing the name of Jacob to Israel. Jacob had gone through many trials in his life, but he never lost sight of God. One night he was in a confrontation with an angel. They wrestled all night and Jacob would not give up the struggle. He had come a long way spiritually and mentally from the days when he had taken the blessing from his brother. He was ready; he had become the man that God could use to build the mighty nation that he had promised to Abram. As the sun was coming up Jacob was blessed by God; his name was changed from Jacob to Israel. By changing his name

[Other nations came about as a result of Abraham, but Israel is the one nation God spoke of in the beginning. Israel came about as a result of his son with Sarah, whose name was Isaac. Then Isaac and Rebekah had Jacob.]

to Israel, it no doubt had a major impact on Jacob. God was sharing his intentions with him and Jacob could now move forward with the same vision as God. God's people became known as Israelites and the name was established. Indeed, Israel became a mighty nation.

We see this name change in the New Testament as well. Jesus had called Simon Barjona by his actual birth name before calling him by his new name.

> And Jesus answered and said unto him, "Blessed art thou, Simon Barjona: for flesh and blood hath not revealed it unto thee, but my Father which is in heaven," (*cf.* Matt. 16:17 KJV).

Simon Bar-jona simply means "Simon son of Jona." Later Jesus referred to him as Peter; "And he brought him to Jesus. And when Jesus beheld him, he said, Thou art Simon the son of Jona: thou shalt be called Cephas, which is by interpretation, a stone," (*cf.* John 1:42 KJV).

[Cephas is Aramaic for stone and Petros is Greek for Rock]

Jesus knew when he looked at Simon that he was looking at a man who had character. He knew that he was looking at a man who was strong enough to follow him. Simon was mentally, emotionally and physically strong enough to follow Jesus through the hardships of their work. And after three years with Jesus, Peter would also possess the spiritual maturity and strength to carry on after Jesus was gone. Simon had some rough edges just like all of us, but Jesus knew he was solid. Jesus called him by his new name, Peter [Petros in Greek]. By calling him Peter, his destiny was being spoken into existence; Peter at first was weak in some areas, but he eventually became that spiritual rock that Jesus saw in him from the beginning.

Many of the people in the Bible had names that were meaningful; they had names that conveyed something to them and to those who addressed them by that name. When we learn to use the power of our words, we can begin to speak things that are not as though they are. When you have a vision, when you begin to see that you have a destiny, you can then begin to speak these things into existence and put them on paper. Then you can apply the action that will propel you forward towards your goals. Align yourself with God's word and your true potential will begin, little by little, to reveal itself. God will share his vision with you for your life.

Breath, Pneuma, Ruah, Spirit

So Jesus said to them again, "Peace to you! As the Father has sent Me, I also send you." And when he had said this, He breathed on them, and said to them, "Receive the Holy Spirit, (*cf.* John 20:21-22 NKJV).

In the English Bible when God spoke to Moses we are told that God is called "Lord." This is not a name, but a title that the translators used. In the Hebrew, God had revealed his name to Moses as "YHVH," which are Hebrew letters pronounced "yod-hey-vav-hey". Over time, people have added vowels to it and have pronounced it as "YAH - WEH," which would change the V to sound more like a W. To vocalize the name "YHVH," breathe in slowly while saying "Yod"—and then breathe out while saying "HEY"—then in again as you breathe "VAV"- then "HEY" as you breathe out. This can only be done by saying it with a breath; when you try it with an audible voice, the pronunciation becomes very difficult to do as you inhale and exhale the sounds. It is much more natural when you do it with a breath [a whisper] rather than with a loud audible voice.

The Lord said, "Go out and stand on the mountain in the presence of the Lord, for the Lord is about to pass by." Then a great and powerful wind tore the mountains apart and shattered the rocks before the Lord, but the Lord was not in the wind. After the wind there was an earthquake, but the Lord was not in the earthquake. After the earthquake came a fire, but the Lord was not in the fire. And after the fire came a gentle "whisper." When

Elijah heard it, he pulled his cloak over his face and went out and stood at the mouth of the cave. Then a voice said to him, "What are you doing here, Elijah, (cf. 1 Kings 19:11–13 NIV).

A teacher by the name of Arthur Waskow said, "Rather than trying to pronounce the name as "Yahweh," try it with no vowels like this, Yyyyhhhhwwwwhhhh; and do this in a whisper or as a breath. The breath of life, God as ruakh ha'olam—breath or spirit of the world. We breathe in what the trees breathe out; and the trees breathe in what we breathe out. [We exchange oxygen and carbon-dioxide.] We are all, both man and nature, dependent on this breath of life. "Some ancient rabbis taught that the name of God was ineffable, an unnamable name, an unspeakable word. They taught that God's name was actually the sound of breath. Pastor Rob Bell of the emergent Mars Hill church suggested this: "When we are born the first thing we have to do is breathe—or say the name of God. The last thing we do when we die is stop breathing—or stop saying the name of God." Even when atheists say things like, "there is no God," they are inadvertently saying his name with every breath. God cannot be denied whether we realize it or not.

Some pro-abortionists argue this point in their favor. They contend that since life doesn't begin until a baby breathes, as some Jewish rabbis and Christian theologians alike have taught; then abortion is not wrong since the baby is not breathing in the sense that we breathe; therefore it is not living in the way that we view life. So, with that in place, is the baby in the womb actually a living person? Do we have to be breathing to be considered alive?

Anything that is alive is constantly growing and changing in one way or another. The baby is alive from the point of conception; from a fertilized egg, to an embryo, to a fetus. From the very first step in the process, this new life is changing, growing and manifesting into his or her destiny. This baby may not take in oxygen exactly the way we do, but nonetheless this is life. Not to be alive is to go the other direction; death results in decay, not growth. So yes, the child in the womb is very much alive. And no, we do not have to breathe to be considered alive or [at least not during our life in the womb].

For there to be a new beginning there will always have to be some type of ending. When we experience changes in life something will always be left behind. When we first start out as a child in the womb, we are in a different world and totally dependent on our mother. Although we do not "breathe" as some would define the word, we are still growing and maturing into something more than what we already are. Once we are born the world inside our mother's womb is left behind. Once we are in this new world or new life, the first thing we must do to live, is to breathe. The fluids that brought us life in the womb will now be taken away, so that our lungs can take in oxygen and begin the process of breathing. We are now experiencing a new reality and a new life. We are now in the place that God told us to subdue, the place where he instructed us to be fruitful and multiply. We have now left one form of life and have entered into a new one.

This is the place or the life where some teach that we begin to say the name of God on our lips as we breathe in and out. No matter what we do or what we say we are speaking the name of God with every breath: his name is on our breath and he is the breath of life. We are dependent on this breath of life to live. We speak words with our breath that should bring life to others. Genesis 2:7 tells us that God breathed the breath of life into the man's nostrils and he came to life. God breathed his breath of life, and both man and nature depend on it to exist.

As we grow and mature in this life, some of us will experience a form of death and then another form of life.

A part of us will die, as something old is ending, to make room for a new beginning. Most of you reading have become a Christian at some point in time. When you did this you became reborn; you have a new life and a new identity through Jesus. Our old self with its desires has died; we are to let that old life we were living die along with our ego and lust. We now have a new reality and new possibilities. Our old way of thinking and living is daily being left behind by the renewing of our mind. Our purpose in life and our potential have now hit high gear and the possibilities are infinite.

At some point, we will experience another loss in the form of physical death; this will be followed by a permanent reality, which is "eternal life."

When we become a born-again Christian we are new creatures in Christ. The fruit of our lips is the most powerful weapon we posses, second only to love. These are two edges of the same sword, (cf. James 3:9). If you truly have love in your heart, the words you speak will reflect that love. In Matthew 12:34 remind us that out of the abundance of the heart the mouth speaks.

By now you may be asking, what in the world does the name of God and breath have to do with the words we speak? When we speak words from our mouth, we do so by the air that crosses over our vocal cords causing vibration to produce different sounds [Our voice is literally our instrument]. If the name of God is in our breath, then this places a whole new importance on the words we speak. Before we say something rude, hateful, or destructive, it would be wise to pause, because it is very possible in the very same breath that we hurt others we are also speaking the name of God. God is life. He is the breath of life. When we use our words to communicate, we should strive to say things that build up, that edify, that restore—words that breathe life into others and inspire them. Always try to speak truth; the truth can hurt, but it can also bring light into a dark situation. The truth has within itself the ability to turn someone's life around. The truth is brought forth with words. I tell you the truth, your voice is your instrument, so let your words be music to the ears of God and to those around you.

And the Lord God formed Man of the dust of the ground, and breathed into his nostrils the breath of life; and man became a living being, (*cf.* Gen. 2:7 NKJV).

Show me, O Lord, my life's end and the number of my days; let me know how fleeting is my life. You have made my days a mere handbreadth; the span of my years is as nothing before you. Each man's life is but a breath. Selah, (*cf.* Psalm 39:4-5 NIV)

IF AGE IMPARTED
WISDOM
THERE WOULDN'T BE
ANY OLD FOOLS.

—Origin Unknown

11
✎Wisdom✎

She is more precious than rubies:
and all the things thou can desire
are not to be compared to her.
Length of days are in her right hand:
and in her left hand riches and honour.
Her ways are ways of pleasantness,
and all her paths are peace.
She is a tree of life to them that lay hold upon her:
and happy is everyone that retaineth her.

Proverbs 3:15-18 KJV

Finding our talents, our purpose and our potential is to share Gods vision for our life. This entire book has been about growing in different areas of our life so that he can guide us to the things he desires for us. As we mature spiritually, mentally and emotionally, we will develop the discipline and the tools we need to keep reaching our potential; wisdom will begin to dwell with us and to be a part of every decision we make. She will manifest herself to us and others by the words we speak, the decisions we make and the people we help along the way.

Most gracious heavenly Father, we pray that you will forgive us of our sins as we forgive not only those who have sinned against us, but we also forgive ourselves for our past mistakes. We ask, dear God, that you guide us in everything we do. Give us eyes to see and ears to hear and not just to see and hear, but to *shema*; to see and to hear and to obey. We ask, Lord, that like Solomon, you bestow some of your wisdom upon us. Show us, Father, how to recognize our gifts and our talents so that they may be used to glorify you, that through our example others will be led to you. Give us the strength to lose ourselves so that we may be found. As we grow and mature help us to keep in mind that we are servants and the best leaders are those who know how to serve. Not our will Father, but Your will be done. In Jesus name, Amen.

"The fear of the Lord is the beginning of wisdom: a good understanding have all they that do *his commandments*: his praise endureth for ever," (*cf.* Psalm 111:10 KJV).

Wisdom can mean different things to different people. In order to renew our mind and improve our life, there must be a certain amount of wisdom; after all, it's wisdom that allows us to see that our lives need improvement in the first place. There is no such thing as perfection, but we can always improve.

A philosopher once said, wisdom brings you in harmony with God. But in reality you can't have wisdom without God. Just as God is light and God is love he is also wisdom; they are intertwined and they are inseparable, it's impossible to have one without the other. Wisdom is older than time itself. Genesis tells us that in the beginning [time] God created the heavens [space] and the earth [matter]. Before this there was only eternity and wisdom dwelt there with God.

The Lord brought me forth as the first of his works, before his deeds of old; I was appointed from eternity, from the beginning, before the world began. When there were no oceans, I was given birth, when there were no springs abounding with water; before the mountains were settled in place, before the hills, I was given birth, before he made the earth or its fields or any of the dust of the world. I was there when he set the heavens in place, when he marked out the horizon on the face of the deep, when he established the clouds above and fixed securely the fountains of the deep, when he gave the sea its boundary so the waters would not overstep his command, and when he marked out the foundations of the earth. Then I was the craftsman at his side. I was filled with delight day after day, rejoicing always in his presence, rejoicing in his whole world and delighting in mankind. "Now then, my sons, listen to me; blessed are those who keep my ways. Listen to my instruction and be wise; do not ignore it. Blessed is the man who listens to me, watching daily at my doors, waiting at my doorway. For whoever finds me finds life and receives favor from the Lord. *But whoever fails to find me harms himself all who hate me love death,* (*cf.* Proverbs 8:22-36 NIV). **[Emphasis added]**

This passage speaks of wisdom—she speaks of herself as "me," which is a living being! The word tells us she was a craftsman. She was full of delight and rejoiced because she was in the presence of God. Wisdom is a living thing, which cannot be obtained in the sense that knowledge, or intelligence can be obtained. Both knowledge and intelligence can be had through education or experience, but wisdom is something that lives inside of you as a result of your relationship with God. An ungodly person can have a high amount of intelligence through education, or they may have a large amount of knowledge in any particular subject. An ungodly person may even have an enormous amount of knowledge concerning the Bible, yet at the same time not possess any wisdom because they chose to live a life outside of the will of God, which is not wise. Don't think that simply knowing the Bible will make you wise. Reading and learning the Bible is a good thing, we all should do it. But some Christians are caught up reading the Bible as though God is a subject to master like algebra or biology. We have to guard against this and come to the realization that what we read in the Bible we must also apply to our life. Knowing what the Bible says does not make us wise; what makes us wise is doing what it says. A.W. Tozer once said, "The devil is a better theologian than any of us and is a devil still," and we know the devil is not wise.

As you draw closer to God, wisdom will begin to dwell inside of you. If you turn your back on God, wisdom will leave you, simply for the fact that wisdom cannot dwell where God is not welcome. She rejoices in his presence. Although you retain your knowledge and education concerning the things of this world, wisdom will start to withdraw herself from you and you'll begin to detect her absence by the poor decisions you make in your life and the fruit that you bear.

> How long will you simple ones love your simple ways? How long will mockers delight in mockery and fools hate knowledge? If you had responded to my rebuke, I would have poured out my heart to you and made my thoughts known to you. But since you rejected me when I called and no one gave heed when I stretched out my hand, since you ignored all my advice and would not accept my rebuke, I in turn will laugh at your disaster; I will mock when calamity overtakes you—when calamity overtakes you like a storm, when disaster sweeps over you like a whirlwind, when distress and trouble overwhelm you. "Then they will call to me but I will not answer; they will look for me but will not find me. Since they hated knowledge and did not choose to fear the Lord, since they would not accept my advice and spurned my rebuke, they will eat the fruit of their ways and be filled with the fruit of their schemes. For the waywardness of the simple will kill them, and the complacency of fools will destroy them; but whoever listens to me will live in safety and be at ease, without fear of harm," (cf. Prov. 1:22-33 (NIV).

Wisdom, according to the Bible, is alive and the Bible refers to wisdom in feminine pronouns: she and her: "at the head of the noisy streets she cries out, in the gateways of the city she makes her speech," (cf. Prov. 1:20 NIV).

It is very interesting the Bible refers to wisdom as a woman, when with few exceptions the Bible is dominated by men. Jesus respected women on a higher level than the men of his day did. It is written that man was created in the image of God. We, as men, are the masculine image of God. It is my opinion that women are his feminine image. Not in the sense that we as people, or the world thinks of masculine and feminine, but in a whole different way. I'm referring to feminine in the way we think, feel and approach life. When a Christian man and a Christian woman come together as husband and wife; they become one flesh and represent the Characteristics of God.

Although Solomon and many men were blessed with large amounts of wisdom; according to the Bible wisdom is a feminine characteristic of God. Maybe this is why it's said that behind every great man is an even greater woman. Intelligence, education, knowledge and understanding are all good things as long as they are achieved through wisdom, which is the will of God.

We are all born with a little bit of wisdom simply because we were created by God in the image of God. This inborn wisdom we could call common sense. A better term might be common wisdom. Common wisdom [or common sense] is the ability to see the consequences of your actions before you act. The Merriam-Webster online dictionary defines common sense as: "sound and prudent judgment based on a simple perception of the situation or facts." In other words, you actually think about what you are going to do or say; you can think several steps ahead or several years ahead and then make a conscious decision based on what you think the proper results will be.

People with common sense or common wisdom may not be scholars or even have college educations but they possess the ability to make wise decisions concerning their marriage, finances and everyday life. There are people who are highly intelligent with multiple degrees "book smart" who have no common sense whatsoever. They are able to achieve a high degree of education, but cannot make basic decisions concerning everyday life. Most of us probably know someone like this. How much wisdom grows inside of us as we age depends on how close to God we become. We don't just merely become wise as a result of getting older.

Cicero was a Roman philosopher and statesman [106 – 43 BC] who stated, "The function of wisdom is to discriminate between good and evil." Cicero was halfway there because the amount of wisdom within us will also determine which way we will go. Just knowing the difference between good and evil is only half the battle.

There are always going to be people who claim to be wise and will use the word of God for their own gain. Simply knowing the Bible does not guarantee you will have any wisdom. And spiritual opportunists, who use God's word for their advantage, will be known by their fruit. The wisdom they possess is sometimes referred to as worldly wisdom, but that is actually not wisdom at all—it's just a perverted copy of the original.

Solomon didn't ask God for riches, fame, or victory over his enemies; he simply asked for the wisdom to govern his people. Because of this he became the wisest and wealthiest man who ever lived.

> The king [Solomon] went to Gibeon to offer sacrifices, for that was the most important high place, and Solomon offered a thousand burnt offerings on that altar. At Gibeon the Lord appeared to Solomon during the night in a dream, and God said, "Ask for whatever you want me to give you." Solomon answered, "You have shown great kindness to your servant, my father David, because he was faithful to you and righteous and upright in heart. You have continued this great kindness to him and have given him a son to sit on his throne this very day. "Now, O Lord my God, you have made your servant king in place of my father David. But I am only a little child and do not know how to carry out my duties. Your servant is here among the people you have chosen, a great people, too numerous to count or number. So, give your servant a discerning heart to govern your people and to distinguish between right and wrong. For who is able to govern this great people of yours?" The Lord was pleased that Solomon had asked for this. So, God said to him, "Since you have asked for this and not for long life or wealth for

yourself, nor have asked for the death of your enemies but for discernment in administering justice, I will do what you have asked. I will give you a wise and discerning heart, so that there will never have been anyone like you, nor will there ever be. Moreover, I will give you what you have not asked for—both riches and honor—so that in your lifetime you will have no equal among kings. And if you walk in my ways and obey my statutes and commands as David your father did, I will give you a long life." Then Solomon awoke—and he realized it had been a dream. He returned to Jerusalem, stood before the ark of the Lord's covenant and sacrificed burnt offerings and fellowship offerings. Then he gave a feast for all his court, (*cf.* 1 Kings 3:4-15 (NIV).

Whether you have a need to improve yourself spiritually, mentally, emotionally, physically or all of the above; if you seek the kingdom of God first (*cf.* Matt. 6:33). God will bless you with wisdom. Through wisdom God will meet your daily needs; each morning you'll awake with grace sufficient for that day (*cf.* 2 Cor. 12:9-10). The thoughts, ideas and opportunities to serve him that you never saw before will suddenly become clear and available. Someone once said, "He will make a way where there is no way. He will bring his peace where there is no peace. He will make a way."

Knowledge and wisdom, far from being one, have often no connection. Knowledge dwells in heads replete with thoughts of other men. Wisdom, in minds attentive to their own knowledge, a rude unprofitable mass, the mere materials with which wisdom builds, till smoothed and squared, and fitted to its place; does encumber whom it seems to enrich. Knowledge is proud that he has learned so much. Wisdom is humble that she knows no more.
— William Cowper [1731 – 1800, English poet]

EVERYTHING IS CREATED
FOR SOME DUTY...
FOR WHAT TASK, THEN,
WERE YOU YOURSELF CREATED?
A MAN'S TRUE DELIGHT
IS TO DO THE THINGS
HE WAS MADE FOR.

—Marcus Aurelius

12
❧ What Is The Purpose Of Life ❧

*Now all has been heard; here is the conclusion of the
matter: Fear God and keep his commandments,
for this is the whole duty of man.*

Ecclesiastes 12:13 NIV

To put away aimlessness and weakness, and to begin to
think with purpose, is to enter the ranks of those strong
ones who only recognize failure as one of the pathways
to attainment; who make all conditions serve them, and
who think strongly, attempt fearlessly, and accomplish
masterfully.
— **James Allen [1864 – 1912, British author and poet]**

What is the purpose to life? Your answer will depend on your
worldview. If you are an atheist, agnostic, or evolutionist
you may not believe in an afterlife or a creator; therefore
you would have a different outlook on the purpose of life
in this world. Although you would probably believe in
kindness to animals and other humans, there would be no
higher power to answer to when you left this life. It stands
to reason that your purpose for living would be whatever
you decide in your mind is right, based on your worldview
and beliefs, plus whatever is socially accepted as decent
behavior.

If you are a Christian, as I am, then there would be a
different worldview and a different set of answers. Since
we as Christians believe in Jesus Christ, then we have to
look beyond ourselves for the purpose to life. What is the
purpose to our life? And why did God create us?

We know that God created us in his image. This means
that we are similar to God and we are his representatives

here on earth. [The Hebrew word for image is *tselem* and the Hebrew word for "likeness" is *demut*, each refer to something that is similar to what it represents. They can also be used to refer to something that represents something else.] And we know that because we are created in his likeness, we also have some of his characteristics. So maybe we should look at the reasons why we as intelligent, mature adults choose to bring children into this world that at times seems to be a great place but at other times can be a very bad place. When we have kids we know they will be in our likeness; that is to say that they will have features from both parents. Even though we hope they inherit all of our best characteristics that will rarely happen. We want to love them and have them love us back. We want to share joy and happiness with them. We want them to enjoy the creation that God has made, whether it's the mountains, the stars, the ocean, animals, art, music, science or many other things they learn about as they grow up. We want to see them grow and learn, fall in love, get married, start a family and become productive members of society. Be fruitful [work] and multiply...

When children first come into this world we picture them living a long and happy life free from pain and sorrow, but we know they will make mistakes. We just hope they learn from their mistakes and move on to better things. It brings us joy to see our children succeed, to be mentally, emotionally and physically well balanced as well as spiritually strong. It makes us sad to see them hurt or to fail at something or to constantly have to struggle through life.

Could it be that this is similar to how God looks at us? He created the universe. He then created us in his likeness. He wanted to share the earth with us; he told us to go out and subdue it. He wants to see us accomplish things, to constantly move ahead and to be better people today than we were yesterday, to be fruitful [work] and multiply, to have love, joy and happiness.

In the beginning, God created us to live forever and not to know sickness or death. Certainly he must have known that sooner or later we would be corrupted, make some mistakes [sin] and that some of us would learn from our mistakes [repent] and move on to be productive and live a life of happiness through God's love and mercy, while others would be rebellious and go through life the hard way.

Christians in the past were wrong to say Christians should be poor and suffer for God's sake. He expects more out of us than that. We were created to glorify him in everything we do. We should always strive to move ahead in life and to accomplish great things, all the while putting God first so that the glory of our accomplishments will be His. If we don't flourish and be diligent with our finances, health, emotions and mind then we will become stagnant and will never be any better off than we are right now, which would be a poor example for people who believe in God to send out to people who don't. We were given abundant life. We should live it to the fullest. To stop growing and moving forward is to start dying. If we as people who believe in God are always struggling just to get by, only living week to week, then how can we help those who are less fortunate than us as God expects? How can we stand here and tell them about the blessings God wants to share with us, if we don't exhibit those things in our own life? We will actually become the less fortunate and the rest of the world will have to help us. That's not much of a life or an example.

We should try to flourish in every aspect of our life so that we can not only help others but also set a good example. When we do good to someone less fortunate than ourselves, we are doing good to God. When we do something for someone else, we are doing God's will.

The King will reply, 'I tell you the truth, whatever you did for one of the least of these brothers of mine, you did for me,' (cf. Matt. 25:40 NIV).

This will bring joy to God just as it would bring us joy to see our children doing the same. By doing these things, we are serving our purpose in life. We are here for a short time to love and to flourish and to do God's will. To live each and every day to our full potential in Christ, to see to it that everything we do in life will be to glorify him. We were created for his glory, to fully understand that and then create a plan of action that aligns itself with that concept, is to find the purpose to life.

13
∽Individual Purpose∾

I cry out to God Most High,
to God who will fulfill (his purpose) for me.

Psalm 57:2 NIV

I am here for a purpose and that purpose is to grow into a mountain, not to shrink to a grain of sand. Henceforth will I apply all my efforts to become the highest mountain of all and I will strain my potential until it cries for mercy.
— **Og Mandino [1923 – 1996 American author]**

The previous chapter addressed the purpose to life in regards to humanity as a whole, but what about us as individuals? God made each of us unique and we each have our very own set of talents and gifts with which he blessed us. We each have our very own calling. We each have our own unique way of doing and saying things that can be used to bless others.

Before we were conceived, God placed within us a destiny. But I believe that each of us have more than one potential, more than one destiny. And we have more than one purpose. In this life, we will never achieve just one purpose, or one destiny. We will have more than one potential as well!

In the grand scheme of things, we have one ultimate purpose and destiny, which is to serve God and bring glory to him. We have the potential to do that. We also have the potential to keep doing it, to get better at it and finding new ways to do it, as we grow older through life. This is where potential comes in. We have the potential to keep glorifying him and doing his work in different ways. We can continually change our realities in life by constantly moving forward. When Jesus was crucified, do you think that he had accomplished all that he could? Certainly not, he could have continued to perform miracles, but he was here on a mission. He came so that through him we would have eternal life. He trained others to carry on his work after he was gone. His job here had to culminate in the crucifixion so that prophecy would be fulfilled. His work continues as he is the intercessor on our behalf (*cf.* Rom. 8:34). He also said he had to go and prepare a place (*cf.* John 14:1-4). His work continues, and like him, our work continues. The work you and I have to do does not stop with only a few accomplishments.

When we become a Christian our purpose in life is to serve God and to see to it that we glorify him in all that we do. But we also have other purposes on a smaller scale. When we get married one of our purposes is to be the best spouse we can be. When we have children, we should make it our purpose to be the best parent we can be. When we take a job, no matter how bad the work is or how little the pay is, our purpose as a Christian is to be the best employee we can possibly be, simply because we are representing Christ and what he stands for. Anything worth doing is worth doing right. We will have many purposes during the course of our life, some will be bigger than others, but each one will serve a purpose.

We do not have just one potential; our potential never ends. If you decide you want to be a nurse you enroll in nursing school. You begin to attend classes and every day you learn something new. You have the potential to become a nurse as long as you study and work hard to achieve the goal. Finally, one day you graduate and you get a job and now you are a nurse. So now being a nurse is no longer your potential; you have already achieved this. Now your potential is going to be something beyond being a nurse, it will be something more.

Let us say that you have decided to become a plumber. You attend trade school or sign on as an apprentice at a plumbing company. You are not a plumber yet, but you possess the potential to become one. Through hard work and a positive attitude you will one day be a licensed plumber if you stay with it and do the work. When you finally go to the state and pass your exam you will then be a plumber. So now becoming a plumber is no longer your potential because you have already accomplished it. Your potential now is something beyond being a plumber. Now you may decide to start your own plumbing company and be a businessman. Once you've established your own business that potential has been fulfilled and you have a new potential that is bigger and better than your business. Your new potential may be to get involved in local politics, or to write a book, or whatever it is God is calling you to do. The point is that once you achieve some type of success and reach a certain plateau that does not mean you have reached your potential, it just means you have realized your potential on that level; now it is time to move to another level because God always has more for you.

We do not have to keep building on the same things in our life. As a matter of fact, God will usually move us around many times during the course of our lives. If we are living in his will and listening and watching for him to guide our steps, we will achieve our potential in one area only to move to another potential in a different area of our life. Every place that he leads us is geared towards fulfilling our destiny in life. No matter where he leads us, we should do his work with purpose because his work will always have a purpose.

God has a purpose and he has a plan. We need to grow to a level of maturity spiritually, mentally and emotionally so that he can share with us his vision for our lives. He shared his plans with Abraham, He shared them with Jacob and he wants to share it with us, too. Sometimes we get caught up in our minds and in material things to the point we do not hear him. Each of us will get off track from time to time because we are human and we are flawed, but if we do our best to stay focused on him, then he will send the Holy Spirit to redirect our steps when we go astray. Just like when Paul tried to take off to Asia, God had to redirect him. It does not matter what plans you try to make, or how many mistakes you make, God will always carry out his purpose. If you fall down, get back up. Les Brown says, "When you fall down try to land on your back, because if you can look up you can get up!"

In Proverbs we are told, "Many are the plans in a man's heart, but it is the Lord's purpose that prevails," Proverbs 19:21 (NIV). I've heard this paraphrased, "Man proposes, God disposes." It's true! The important thing to remember is when you make mistakes and fall short of his expectations for your life, it is ok. Just always come back to him and he will use your mistakes to carry out your destiny anyway.

And we know that in all things God works for the good of those who love him, who have been called according to his purpose, (*cf.* Romans 8:28 NIV).

Our life is about seasons. Seasons come and go; when one season of your life is over there is another one waiting. With each new season there will come a new purpose, a new potential and new possibilities. Just as we have many seasons throughout our lives we do not have just one potential, but many.

And there were also many other things that Jesus did, which if they were written one by one, I suppose that even the world itself could not contain the books that would be written. Amen, John 21:25 (NKJV).

Just like Jesus, we are to continually keep realizing our potential. Jesus had the potential to do anything, things far greater than what the disciples witnessed. He came here for us. Not only did he die for our sins so that we could have eternal life through him. He lived as an example to us, so that we could see firsthand what is possible through him. He wants us not only to have life, but to have it more abundantly. Jesus did many wonderful things but one of the greatest things he did, was to overcome death and the grave. And through him we have the potential to do the same.

FAILURE IS A DETOUR,
NOT A DEAD-END STREET.

—Zig Ziglar

14

⤚Forget Your Past Failures⤙

Brethren, I do not regard myself as having laid hold of it
yet; but one thing I do:
forgetting what lies behind and reaching forward
to what lies ahead.

Philippians 3:13 NIV

Therefore everyone who hears these words of mine and puts them into practice is like a wise man who built his house on the rock. The rain came down, the streams rose, and the winds blew and beat against that house; yet it did not fall, because it had its foundation on the rock. But everyone who hears these words of mine and does not put them into practice is like a foolish man who built his house on sand. The rain came down, the streams rose, and the winds blew and beat against that house, and it fell with a great crash," (*cf.* Matthew 7:24-27 NIV).

Jesus spoke a parable about the wise man who built his home on a rock; and the foolish man who built his home on sand. When the storms came, the house built on the rock stood strong. The house built on sand was destroyed and washed away. Jesus never told us that this was one good man and one bad man. He didn't say that one of them was evil and the other holy. He just simply let us know that one was wise and one was foolish. These were probably two very nice men for all we know. They both were probably good and decent people; one of the men simply made a bad decision.

We as Christians should grow in every aspect of our life. We are no longer supposed to stumble around blind; we now have eyes that should be opened to the life that God desires for us. C. S. Lewis stated, "I believe in Christianity as I believe the sun has risen, not only because I see it—but because by it, I can see everything else."

Even though we are Christians and no longer living and walking in darkness, some of us either do not or cannot see clearly sometimes. Each of us has been guilty of making foolish decisions and doing foolish things in our lives; just like the man who built on sand. Perhaps he fell in love with things that appealed to his flesh—things he heard, things he felt and things he saw. Rather than keeping these "things" well balanced, he allowed his emotions to override his wisdom, which caused him to ignore his foundation.

Now the wise man had a thought first; he had the ability to take this thought and imagine in his mind what he was going to build. He would fast and go to God in prayer before he started to build, seeking God's guidance and wisdom.

Because his mind had been renewed and he sought out God first, he was blessed with the wisdom to realize that the foundation was the most important thing to consider before he started building his house. Later, after his house was built and the storms of life came, and the house withstood them. Then, he could step back and behold what he had created to see that it was good. He could then rejoice and experience the emotions evoked by this good thing he built.

The foolish man lost his home...but he does not have to lose hope. He can now start over and learn from his mistake. He can now start fresh with a new foundation and a new house. When he does this, he will also get a new identity; he will no longer be identified as "the foolish man." He will now be identified as a wise man with a solid foundation.

You and I are both the wise man and the foolish man. Our life is our house. We decide whether the foundation of our life is strong like an immovable rock, or weak like shifting sand. We decide this by everything that we say, the way we act in different situations, the way we think and our philosophy of life.

Being wise and building our life on the solid foundation of Christ is to be like the tree that bares good fruit. Everything that is alive is healthy and grows; it becomes more mature and stronger year after year. If we plant a fruit tree, if it is healthy and full of life, will mature and grow each year and produce fruit. This tree will be known and identified by the fruit it produces. Is the fruit good and healthy attracting those who come to it? Or is it bad and toxic, causing people to turn away?

To be healthy and whole is to grow. To stop growing and living is to start dying. We are all a part of nature and our life is similar to what goes on in nature. If we slow down, take a look, just be present and listen; we can discern these similarities. In the Bible, our lives are compared to fruit trees, rock, sand and nature. We are all God's creation; man and nature are representative of each other.

We need a solid foundation based on God: we need to be well rooted in his word. Once we have established our foundation—our core principals and beliefs—growth does not stop, it is always just beginning. We are to grow stronger and draw closer to God year after year. By doing this we will realize our potential in life. We will begin to see our talents and invest them wisely. We want our talents to multiply because they are not really ours; they are on loan to us from God. They belong to our Master and he wants them to be invested and multiplied, not buried. When he returns he may ask us what we did with the talents he entrusted to us. As of right now—at this very moment in your life—what would your answer be?

It does not matter how many times you were the foolish man. No matter how many failures you have experienced during the course of your life, God wants you to know that you can start fresh. Forget past failures and mistakes. Learn from them and experience new growth. As a result of your willingness to see, to hear, and to do, you are now becoming the wise man or woman, building your foundation on the rock.

When we finally decide to step out and to take an active role in the world by losing ourselves, that's when we will finally discover who we are. When we decide to give up our own life, that's when we will find life in abundance. Then we'll finally discover the talents with which our master has blessed each one of us. When we become a new person through Christ, we will have a new identity. By staying in the word and praying daily we will begin to understand what it means to have an intimate relationship with God. As we grow and mature spiritually it's going to have a profound effect on the way we view this world, as well as everyone and everything in it. The more we are blessed, the more we get, the more we should give. Whatever we receive is not ours, but his who bestowed it upon us. We are to invest in the success of others as we grow in Christ. We are to be a good example to others so that they will want what we have. When they ask about the joy inside of us we are to be prepared to give an answer.

> But in your hearts set apart Christ as Lord. Always be prepared to give an answer to everyone who asks you to give the reason for the hope that you have. But do this with gentleness and respect, (*cf.* 1 Pet. 3:15 NIV).

Someone once said, "It's better to be prepared for an opportunity before it comes, than it is to have an opportunity come and not be prepared." As we develop our spiritual lives and mature emotionally and mentally, we will reap a life full of blessings as a result of our growth.

"We don't get out of life what we want. We get out of life what we are" This, to me, is a beautiful statement because even though we do not always get what we want, we can always change who we are. When we change who we are for the better, then our life becomes better.

Several years ago I realized that in order to be the man God wants me to be I had to begin with myself. I had to start from scratch and rebuild my mind. In order to inspire others we have to renew our minds and our vocabulary so that we can allow God, through the Holy Spirit, to lead us into our destiny and our true potential. So many of us pray for a better job, a loving spouse, a nice home, a raise in pay and many other things. God wants these things for us, but what are we doing to bring them about? We are responsible for our half of the whole. God wants us to be whole, but not if it means he has to do all of the work. We have to do our part. If we want success in our life, then we must invest in the success of others. If you want that loving spouse, that better job, or that nice home, you have to improve every area of your life, spiritually, mentally and emotionally so the blessings of God can be given to you in good measure, pressed down, shaken together and running over (cf. Luke 6:38). We are to pursue God and to pursue wisdom and that is it. All of the other good things in life are not to be pursued; they are to be attracted. When we allow the Lord to work in our life and transform us into a new person in Christ. We will attract the good things in life. To go out and pursue them will cause them to flee from before us. God wants us to pursue him and wisdom; everything else we get by making ourselves more attractive. The exception would be an education. Education would not be seen as something we pursue or attract; it's something we achieve as a result of God's wisdom and guidance.

If you desire a better job then you have to improve your skills so potential employers are attracted to your abilities. Do the things necessary to make yourself qualify for that new job.

If you are seeking a husband or a wife, but you have anger and negativity from your last relationship, then how in the world can you bring anything of value to a new relationship until you resolve those problems? Get rid of the anger by forgiving; forget the negativity by focusing on living in the moment instead of in your past. Make sure you are not looking to another person as your source of happiness; the only source you need is God. Get a new and improved attitude; change your vocabulary from nasty and negative to powerful and positive. When we enact these changes we will begin to attract the things in life God wants for our destiny: a better job, a husband or a wife, a nicer home and a strong network of Christian friends to fellowship with.

We can do this! We can show every person that enters our life how to do it as well. Let us hear the master say upon his return: "...Well done, good and faithful servant! You have been faithful with a few things; I will put you in charge of many things. Come and share your master's happiness!," (*cf.* Matt. 25:21 NIV).

Conclusion:

Decide right now, at this very moment, to seek God and to see him in everything you do. Resolve to be conscious of him everywhere you go. Know that you are never alone no matter what the circumstances may be. Allow him to be your teacher. He has placed a desire in my heart and in yours to learn; to allow him to educate us, to reveal to us a better understanding of him and what he desires. But it is not only about me or you—it's about sharing my journey with you, and having you share your journey with others, and all of us growing together. We each possess potential. We each have gifts and talents that he gave us. Our job is to discover what they are. By seeking him, our purposes in life will be made known to us through the Holy Spirit. My goal in life is to be better every day than I was the day before. This is what God wants for me and for you.

My goal with this book is to pique your interest enough that you become motivated. Motivated to dig deeper and to go beyond what is written in these pages. To find out what God wants from you and for you. To accomplish more in life than you ever thought possible, and in return to allow thanks, credit and the glory to be His. Everything you accomplish will not be your accomplishments, but his, so that God can work through you, so that he can put it into the hearts of those around you to want what you have.

We should strive to be better every single day than we were the day before. And we should repeat this every single day until the day we die. Step out of your comfort zone and expand yourself to the point you can feel the stretch marks on your mind and spirit. Get involved in life and strive to reach your full potential in Christ!

CPSIA information can be obtained at www.ICGtesting.com
Printed in the USA
LVOW070258160113

315772LV00001B/34/P